The Sunday Telegraph
General Knowledge
Crossword Book

The Sunday Telegraph
General Knowledge
Crossword Book

Pan Books
in association with *The Sunday Telegraph*

First published 1999 by Pan Books

an imprint of Pan Macmillan Ltd
Pan Macmillan, 20 New Wharf Road, London N1 9RR
Basingstoke and Oxford
Associated companies throughout the world
www.panmacmillan.com

In association with *The Sunday Telegraph*

ISBN 0 330 39134 8

20 19 18 17 16 15 14 13 12 11

A CIP catalogue record for this book is available from the
British Library.

Printed in Great Britain by
Mackays of Chatham plc, Chatham, Kent

1

ACROSS

1 European bunting with brown streaked wings and tail (12)
8 Stop or cover a cavity or opening (7)
9 Factory where skins and hides are treated (7)
11 Loch near The Trossachs in central Scotland (7)
12 Person's usual haunt (7)
13 Piece of gummed paper used by philatelists (5)
14 Swallowing up completely (9)
16 Inflammation of the sensitive layer of the eye (9)
19 Malay sailing-boat (alternative spelling) (5)
21 Claw that is bent like a sickle (7)
23 Poor man's one possession (3-4)
24 The music for this old French dance often occurs in suites (7)
25 Animal that lives on the surface of another (7)
26 Scottish athlete who was the Sports Writers' Sportswoman of the Year in 1989 (6,6)

DOWN

1 State and peninsula in SE Mexico (7)
2 Silicate of aluminium and potassium, a whitish 5 down (7)
3 Force oneself to work too hard (9)
4 Angry, overexcited (3,2)
5 Substance that's not animal, vegetable or abstract (7)
6 People who have been honourably discharged from public duties (7)
7 Tall grass with greyish-green leaves covered with soft hair (9,3)
10 Sir Francis —— , British explorer mainly in North India and Tibet (12)
15 In Canada, the alewife, a type of herring (9)
17 Israeli city which incorporated Jaffa in 1950 (3,4)
18 Minute organisms found floating or swimming on the water's surface (7)
19 Person of chief rank or office (7)
20 Science of bodily structure (7)
22 White poplar-tree (5)

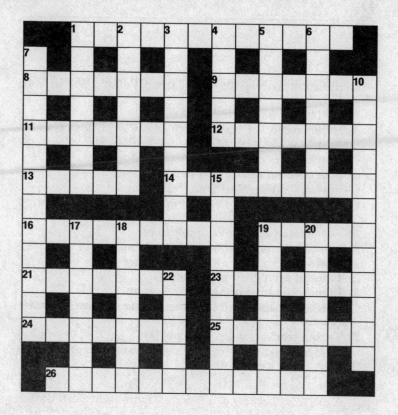

ACROSS

1 Singer who had the hit *Harper Valley PTA* in 1968 (7,1,5)
7 Building used for storage (5)
8 Inflammation of bone cavity in the skull that communicates with the nose (9)
9 Another name for sulphuric acid (7)
10 Sports arena with tiered seats (7)
11 Port in Antrim, Northern Ireland (5)
12 Small piece of land rented out for private cultivation (9)
14 —— Water, lake in W Cumbria (9)
17 —— Mohammad, batsman and captain of Pakistan 1964-7 (5)
19 Place of privacy or seclusion (7)
21 Plant's climbing organ (7)
22 Green deposit which forms on copper, bronze and brass (9)
23 Tartan trousers worn by Scots (5)
24 Central character of a short rhyme concerning the days of the week (7,6)

DOWN

1 Planet fifth from the sun (7)
2 Sitting, as on a horse, with a leg on either side (7)
3 County town of Co. Clare (5)
4 Recommence or begin again (7)
5 Lavatory found in a camp (7)
6 Series of cascades in National Park of the same name in California (8,5)
7 Former Radio 1 DJ who announced his resignation during his programme (4,3,6)
8 Small, pale, seedless raisin (7)
13 In Greek mythology, the father of Odysseus (7)
15 One with an aptitude for a particular activity (7)
16 Metallic element with symbol Re (7)
17 Devon town famous for lace-making (7)
18 Room for young children (7)
20 Capital of Piedmont region of Italy (5)

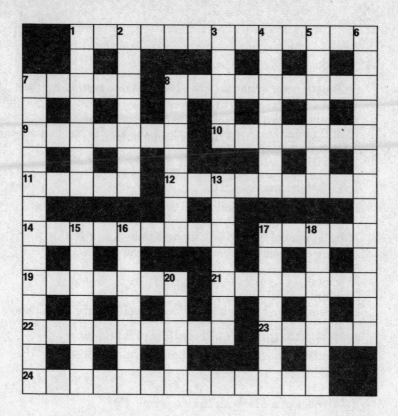

ACROSS

1 Fourth compartment of the stomach of a ruminant (8)
5 Grammatical structure in sentences (6)
8 Scottish word for a small cup (6)
9 Person who eats the flesh of other humans (8)
10 Leguminous plant cultivated for its edible seeds (8)
11 Numbed, with a prickly or tingling feeling (6)
12 Tree-dwelling rodent (8)
13 Prefix meaning deceptively resembling (6)
15 Characteristic of country-dwellers (6)
18 Ball-game played with long, hooked sticks (8)
20 Issue of a periodical or serial (6)
21 Recently married (5-3)
23 Box in which the ship's compass is kept (8)
24 It is used to secure a head-covering to one's hair (6)
25 Japanese sport of unarmed combat (6)
26 Matter that settles at the bottom of liquid (8)

DOWN

1 Member of a Mexican Indian people (5)
2 Person who enjoys hurting himself or herself (9)
3 Footballer in front of goalkeeper assisting in defence (7)
4 Donald Swann's singing partner (7,8)
5 Fleshy multiple fruit formed from several flowers (7)
6 Dramatic picture or scene (7)
7 Musical instrument played with hard-headed hammers (9)
12 This S African antelope moves in leaps when alarmed (9)
14 Self-contained community of plants, animals & their physical environment (9)
16 Short intensive course of study (7)
17 Small, roundish rowing-boat (7)
19 Alternative name for a byre (7)
22 Shorter spelling for a small fried cake (5)

)

4

ACROSS

1 Surgeon's instrument, a bone-scraper (6)
4 Plant with spikes of blue, pink or white spurred flowers (8)
8 Resinous oily substance (6)
9 A living animal or vegetable (8)
10 Ornamental shrub often called japonica (8)
11 German who initiated the Protestant Reformation (6)
12 Pronounced with emphasis (8)
13 River flowing through Shrewsbury (6)
15 Apple with rough brownish-red skin (6)
18 Branch growing from main stem of a plant (8)
20 Unwholesome or noxious vapour (6)
21 Violation of grammar or etiquette (8)
23 French Calvinist of 16th or 17th century (8)
24 Heavy cylinder for flattening turf (6)
25 Small northern songbird (8)
26 Venerable magician in Arthurian legend (6)

DOWN

1 Small three-masted Mediterranean vessel (5)
2 Not having any flavour (9)
3 Remus's twin brother (7)
4 He played the part of "Reginald Perrin" (7,8)
5 Star of the first magnitude in the constellation Leo (7)
6 "I beseech you", an archaic interjection (7)
7 Dutch painter and etcher 1606-69 (9)
12 Sailor's spare-time handicraft (9)
14 To do with transport (9)
16 Piece of glittering material (7)
17 Person under instruction (7)
19 Pivot on which a lever turns (7)
22 Somewhat feeble-minded person (5)

5

ACROSS

1 The Dalai Lama's homeland (5)
4 Dissertation involving analysis and assessment (8)
8 Female pilot (8)
9 Political stirrer (8)
11 Hebrew God as revealed to Moses (7)
13 Port on Humber estuary NW of Grimsby (9)
15 *Carry On* star who created the character "Rambling Syd Rumpo" (7,8)
18 Another name for the common rorqual (5-4)
21 Longest river in China (7)
22 Motorway with tolls in America (8)
24 Type of brown sugar in large crystals (8)
25 Part of a unit (8)
26 Bristle-like appendages (5)

DOWN

1 Extravagantly sentimental song or film (4-6)
2 Coastal resort adjoining Hove (8)
3 Smarten oneself up (8)
4 Technical name for the hip-bone (4)
5 Check-patterned material worn by Highland clans in Scotland (6)
6 Another name for couch-grass (6)
7 Large jug with a wide spout (4)
10 Designed to attract publicity or attention (8)
12 Seize or divert a vehicle whilst in transit (8)
14 Gathering in which guests wear face-coverings and costumes (10)
16 Thinness or slenderness (8)
17 Condensed summary or abridgement (8)
19 Stockade round village or campsite in Sudan (6)
20 Sound of an explosion (6)
22 Surface of and covered with grass (4)
23 Garden home of Adam and Eve (4)

ACROSS

1 Handbook used for constant reference (4-5)

6 Small shoot or twig (5)

9 Type of sleeveless vest (7)

10 Ornamental should-piece (9)

11 Egg-shaped wind instrument (7)

12 Crude metal produced in a blast furnace (3-4)

13 Church service of thanksgiving in autumn (7,8)

18 Soft greyish-white metallic element (7)

20 Disease carried by mosquitoes (7)

22 One million cycles per second (9)

23 Air-sacs at termination of brachioles in the lungs (7)

24 ——-cake, rich sweet cake (5)

25 Midlands town known for its footwear industry (9)

DOWN

1 Ancient settler in S France and Spain (8)

2 Large extinct reptile (8)

3 Landlocked country of Africa, formerly Nyasaland (6)

4 A chain or connected series (6)

5 American plant with egg-shaped fruit (3-5)

6 Window found in the roof (8)

7 Any bird of prey eg owl or falcon (6)

8 Member of organisation which puts Bibles into hotel bedrooms (6)

14 Christian festival on January 6th (8)

15 Shrub or small tree with feathery clusters of pink or whitish flowers (8)

16 Musicians of the highest technical skill (8)

17 Forming a link (8)

18 Brass percussion instrument (6)

19 Another word for lumberjack (6)

20 His works include *Don Giovanni* (6)

21 National museum and art gallery in Paris (6)

ACROSS

1 Disc-jockey and TV personality (6,9)
9 Courage, heroism (7)
10 Jean ——, French dramatist 1889-1963 (7)
11 Form of gelatine derived from air-bladders of certain fishes (9)
12 Adam ——, Scottish economist and philosopher (5)
13 Rosamond ——, British novelist whose books include *Dusty Answer* (7)
15 French city with famous 12th century bridge which is now partly destroyed (7)
17 Father of Isaac and founder of the Hebrew people (7)
19 Refrigerated ships (slang) (7)
21 Large flat ring used in a game (5)
23 Special treatment given to an important person (3-6)
25 First letter of a word (7)
26 Mark under letter c (7)
27 Series of battles fought between England and France between 1337 and 1453 (7,5,3)

DOWN

1 Archangel, messenger of good news in Daniel and Luke (7)
2 African forest animal closely related to the giraffe (5)
3 Sign or symbol used to represent a word (9)
4 One of Constable's best known paintings (3,4)
5 Capital of Cyprus (7)
6 Bone in the middle ear (5)
7 Dutifulness or submission (9)
8 Eldest son of a French king (7)
14 Person educated at one of the top public schools (9)
16 Person from Reykjavik perhaps (9)
17 Prime minister from 1908-16 (7)
18 Irregularly mottled and streaked (7)
19 Small root or rootlike part (7)
20 Expected to remain fine (3,4)
22 Ancient capital of a Celto-Germanic tribe on river Moselle (5)
24 Highly spiced eastern rice dish (5)

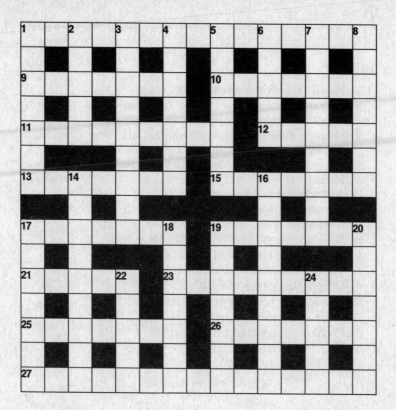

8

ACROSS

1 Small Old World warbler (9)
9 Humorous variant of word meaning to spatter with water or mud (6)
10 Quarrelsome woman, a virago (9)
11 Arc of an eighth of the circumference of a circle (6)
12 Expert or group of experts regarded as a source of ideas (5-4)
13 Secluded or indirect footway (6)
17 Wooden coffer in which Tables of the Law were kept (OT) (3)
19 Elvis Presley's first big hit (10,5)
20 The longest river in Scotland (3)
21 Taking cargo aboard a ship (6)
25 Official language of South Africa (9)
26 The largest tributary of the Hudson River (6)
27 Ballroom dance such as a fast foxtrot (9)
28 Probable, expected to happen (6)
29 Small Old World songbird (9)

DOWN

2 Whitish wood from a large West African tree (6)
3 Oblong, spotted game piece (6)
4 Colloquial word expressing acquiescence (6)
5 Fracture in earth's crust in California (3,7,5)
6 Fourteen books included as an appendix in some Bibles (9)
7 Napolean ——, French emperor 1804-15 (9)
8 Where the main government offices can be found (9)
14 Athenian princess who was transformed into a nightingale in Greek mythology (9)
15 Gesture of welcoming or of agreeing a deal (9)
16 —— Jackson, Confederate general (9)
17 —— Garfunkel, Paul Simon's singing partner (3)
18 Foster brother and steward of King Arthur (3)
22 Tetragonal mineral such as jacinth or jargoon (6)
23 Unit of measurement of distances of stars (6)
24 Guts or alimentary canals in higher animals (6)

9

ACROSS

1 County, port and mountains in Eastern Ireland (7)
5 Constellation in Northern Hemisphere close to Andromeda and Pisces (7)
9 British composer best known for his trilogy *Song of Hiawatha* (9-6)
10 Member of the old royal family of Peru (4)
11 Band of mown grass (5)
12 —— Brummell, a man who set the fashion in men's clothes (4)
15 Instrument for measuring electric current in amperes (7)
16 Incidentally, by the way (7)
17 Petty gangster (7)
19 Wild or half wild horse found in SW USA (7)
21 Narrow strip of wood (4)
22 Organic compound, a derivative of ammonia (5)
23 Port and resort in Southern Portugal (4)
26 Miss Jones in *Rising Damp* (7,2,2,4)
27 Spanish cardinal, statesman and grand inquisitor (7)
28 Omar —— , astronomer and poet noted for the *Rubaiyat* (7)

DOWN

1 City in Southern Kansas in Glen Campbell's 1969 hit —— *Lineman* (7)
2 Novel by Stella Gibbons (4,7,4)
3 Brightly-coloured Australian or Indonesian parrot (4)
4 Man whose wife has passed away (7)
5 Quills for plucking musical instruments (7)
6 Thomas —— , author of *Elegy written in a Country Churchyard* (4)
7 Understandable without any clarification (4-11)
8 Johann —— , Austrian composer (7)
13 Gramophone needles (5)
14 France's chief naval station is based in this port (5)
17 Capital of Nova Scotia (7)
18 Imitation of nature or human behaviour (7)
19 Halfway between today and next Saturday (7)
20 Coarse cloth often stiffened with gum that used to be used for clothing (7)
24 Painted or mosaic image of Christ (4)
25 Jakarta is its capital (4)

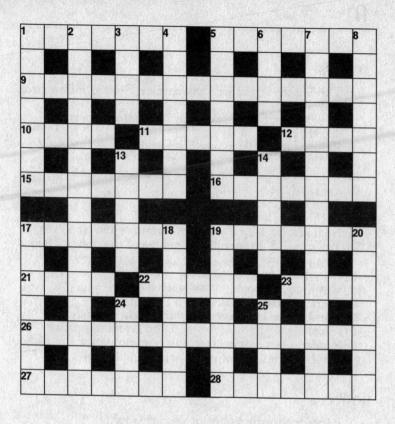

ACROSS

1 Threadlike structure that carries genetic information (10)
6 —— Minor, historical name for Anatolia (part of Turkey) (4)
9 Remove organ from one body and graft it into another (10)
10 Cheese similar to but milder than Camembert (4)
13 Forks of the windpipe (7)
15 John Maynard ——, English economist (6)
16 Rotherham football team (6)
17 He had a hit with *Poetry in Motion* in 1960 (6,9)
18 Town in SW France that's centre of the district famed for its brandy (6)
20 Outermost membrane of the eyeball (6)
21 Old French dance, or music for it (7)
22 French battle of 1590 (4)
25 Dwelling used for secondary or occasional lodging (4-1-5)
26 Sudden blast of wind (4)
27 Great abundance or overflowing supply (10)

DOWN

1 Large town, often one with a cathedral (4)
2 Standard monetary unit of Iran and of Oman (4)
3 Plural of Mr (6)
4 No1 hit for the Tremeloes in 1967 (7,2,6)
5 Member of Mongoloid race in NE China, or their language (6)
7 Scottish dance, similar to a reel, but slower (10)
8 Person from "The Granite City" (10)
11 Commandeering an aircraft in mid-air (10)
12 Greek philosopher and mathematician of sixth century BC (10)
13 Large cushion used as an informal seat (7)
14 Account of goods supplied (7)
19 Unbleached cotton fabric without a printed design (6)
20 Crackling on a vinyl record (6)
23 Homework or period reserved for this (especially in boarding schools) (4)
24 German battle of 1806 (4)

11

ACROSS

1 Mythological strong man (8)
9 Written defence or vindication (8)
10 Alligator —— , the avocado (4)
11 Novel by Leo Tolstoy (4,8)
13 World's second largest ocean (8)
15 Hindu or Sikh festival of lamps (6)
16 River Thames at Oxford (4)
17 Tall coniferous, evergreen tree (5)
18 Russian city on River Irtysh (4)
20 Bowl-shaped recess on mountainside (6)
21 Clownishness or craziness (8)
23 European marshland grass (8-4)
26 Common skin disease of adoloscence (4)
27 Journey a long way across country (8)
28 Administrative centre of Grampian Region in Scotland (8)

DOWN

2 Retired title, especially for a professor (8)
3 Eastern unfurnished inn (12)
4 Flax-seed-eating common finch (6)
5 Dismiss from employment (colloq) (4)
6 Passageway in a train (8)
7 Registered trademark name for a fruit that's a cross between a grapefruit and an orange (4)
8 Ornamental shrub or small tree (8)
12 Part of eastern Canada (12)
14 Seaport in SW Spain (5)
16 The act of cutting in surgery (8)
17 Road on which motorists are not allowed to stop (8)
19 Excitement felt reading a thriller (8)
22 Delicate shade of difference (6)
24 Second-hand (4)
25 Queen of Sparta, mother of Castor and Pollux (4)

ACROSS

1 Wise Old Testament character (7)
5 Deep-red winter apple (4-3)
9 Very fine green tea (5)
10 Fine variety of apple (9)
11 Solid metal printing plate (10)
12 Smooth or legato effect in music (4)
14 Spanish artist whose works include `Guernica' (5,7)
18 Scottish song sung communally (4,4,4)
21 Chinese breed of dog (4)
22 Object produced by a manual art (10)
25 Lower house of German parliament 1867-1933 (9)
26 Essential oil from damask rose (5)
27 Loudspeaker used to produce high-frequency sounds (7)
28 Dame Edith —— , English poet (7)

DOWN

1 Split or division in a church (6)
2 Antiseptic pioneer (6)
3 Resort town in Monaco (5,5)
4 Composition for nine musicians (5)
5 Air-passages from throats to lungs (9)
6 Father of Shem, Ham and Japheth (4)
7 Like some grapes, not having pips (8)
8 Despicable coward (8)
13 Breaker of religious images (10)
15 English city on River Lune (9)
16 French card-game which involves gambling (8)
17 Toothpaste additive (8)
19 Jean Paul —— , French philosopher (6)
20 Waxy insoluble form of alcohol (6)
23 French impressionist painter and sculptor (5)
24 Dull sound of a small explosion (4)

ACROSS

1 Person who is happier not to go out (4-2-4,4)
9 This thinking seeks new ways of looking at problems (7)
10 Water-parsnip with edible roots (7)
11 Pit for collecting oil (4)
12 Italian blue-veined cheese (10)
14 Suitable for growing crops (6)
15 Marriage within one's own tribe (8)
17 One of eight bicuspid teeth in a human adult (8)
18 Town south of Gloucester (6)
21 Arthropod with shell, eg lobster or crab (10)
22 N Indian city, site of the Taj Mahal (4)
24 Thick paste of sugar and water used in sweets (7)
25 Pain in the lower back (7)
26 Mountain no longer liable to erupt (7,7)

DOWN

1 Mainly Polish region in Central Europe (7)
2 This usually falls on September 23rd in Northern Hemisphere (8,7)
3 Distinctive character, subtle emanation (4)
4 In Greek mythology the god of the sun (6)
5 Hatred of women (8)
6 Coastal resort north of Torquay (10)
7 One who is not diplomatically acceptable (7,3,5)
8 Lustful or erotic (6)
13 Clouds forming a continuous layer at 8,000 to 20,000 feet (10)
16 Drug that produces numbness and stupor (8)
17 Mollify, appease (6)
19 Game in which a spinning top is caught on a cord (7)
20 Russian physiologist and physician (6)

23 Alcohol radical C_5H_{11} (4)

ACROSS

8 Genus of mayfly with very short life (8)
9 Ionian island regarded as the home of Homer's Odysseus (6)
10 Household god (3)
11 Embryonic tissue, afterbirth (8)
12 Tropical plant of the spurge family (6)
13 *Twilight of the Gods*, musical drama by Wagner (15)
15 Confound or bewilder (7)
18 Part of horse's foot between fetlock and hoof (7)
21 Tense or stressful relationship (7,8)
24 Large Indian antelope (6)
25 Fabled flower that never fades, emblem of immortality (8)
26 Father of Joshua (OT) (3)
27 British French-born poet who wrote *Cautionary Tales* (6)
28 Brass wind instrument with a slide (8)

DOWN

1 Any of a series of manned US spacecraft (6)
2 Group of three lines rhyming together (6)
3 He painted *The Last Supper* (8,2,5)
4 The most virtuous knight of King Arthur's Round Table (7)
5 One who has sailed round the world (15)
6 Divine or deified ruler (8)
7 Large sherry glass (8)
14 19th letter of Greek alphabet (3)
16 With a network of crossed bars (8)
17 Plant with orange or yellow flowers (8)
19 Unit of work or energy (3)
20 Capital of Georgia (USA) (7)
22 Not far away, close at hand (6)
23 Bell rung in Lloyd's in London before announcement such as the loss of a ship (6)

15

ACROSS

6 Barker and Corbett on TV (3,3,7)

8 French city, capital of Somme department (6)

9 180 degrees meridian from Greenwich (4-4)

10 Beverage served hot or iced (3)

11 Very large edible prawns (6)

12 Pottery with white Cameo relief on (often) blue ground (8)

14 Dialectal word for nevertheless (7)

16 Small town NE of Forres in Grampian Region (7)

20 Percussion instrument shaped like a flat box (8)

23 Billowing white clouds (6)

24 Scottish interjection of surprise (3)

25 Tissue that forms a scar (alternative spelling) (8)

26 Double —— , a stunning blow (6)

27 Kind person who helps another in difficulty (4,9)

DOWN

1 Jesus Christ, the Saviour (8)

2 Nazi's symbol (8)

3 Small boring tool (7)

4 Leeds football team (6)

5 Tree used in the manufacture of cricket bats (6)

6 Taking too long to be worth while (4-9)

7 OT book preceding Isaiah (4,2,7)

13 Type of trap for catching small mammals (3)

15 Broad sash worn with a kimono (3)

17 Looper caterpillar (4-4)

18 Thrash or reprimand severely (alternative spelling) (8)

19 During the next or coming month (7)

21 Former capital of Poland on River Vistula (6)

22 Swampy ground, bog (6)

16

ACROSS

1 Bands of lights seen around the South Pole, the southern lights (6,9)
9 Common descriptive name for a robin (9)
10 Trilling sound some birds and insects make (5)
11 Palace built in 1538 for Henry VIII (7)
12 Country NW of Peru straddling the equator (7)
13 Loch west of Fort William (3)
14 Moved rapidly often noisily or violently (7)
17 This palace is the pope's cathedral church (7)
19 Secret state police in Nazi Germany (7)
22 Black and dark grey Eurasian bird (7)
24 Old French gold or silver coin (3)
25 Silver or pewter mug (7)
26 Capital of Pakistan until 1960 (7)
28 Lower down on the page (5)
29 Press-agent or journalist (9)
30 Greenish-yellow plant of the London pride genus (6,9)

DOWN

1 August Wilmhelmj's arrangement of the 2nd movement of J S Bach's suite No 3 (3,2,3,1,6)
2 French sculptor noted for his portrayal of the human form (5)
3 Finback whale (7)
4 Struck with shame or embarrassment (7)
5 Dame Edith ——, author of Facade in 1922 (7)
6 Alternative spelling for a tennis bat (7)
7 Illegally handled trans- fer of money or goods (9)
8 British inventor of the jet engine (3,5,7)
15 Full of bitterness (9)
16 Telepathic clairvoyance (3)
18 Turkish military commander (3)
20 Rare mineral that con- tains titanium oxide (7)
21 Son of Laius and Jocasta in Greek mythology (7)
22 Slot-machine that plays records (4-3)
23 Large city in South Glamorgan (7)
27 Third largest country in the world (5)

17

ACROSS

1 Operetta by Gilbert and Sullivan (5,2,4)
10 Someone to whom money is paid (5)
11 Having no value (9)
12 Brittle silvery-white element obtained from gold, silver and copper ore (9)
13 Hittite officer who was married to Bathsheba (5)
14 American word for a rocky ravine or dry watercourse (6)
16 Stately or sublime (8)
18 Seaside resort in Somerset (8)
20 Rhyming game (6)
23 Franz —— , Hungarian composer (5)
24 American word for a catapult (9)
26 Cause to sprout, begin to grow (9)
27 —— Gras, (Shrove Tuesday) (5)
28 Fifth book of the Bible (11)

DOWN

2 Befitting a king or queen (5)
3 In Wiltshire, it is the site of England's largest megalithic monument (7)
4 Express grief or mourn loudly (6)
5 Lamentation, a tale of grief (8)
6 Provide new accommodation (7)
7 Scientific study of the eye (13)
8 In succession, one after another (8)
9 Genus of plants including the Californian poppy (13)
15 Owner or manager of a large farm in Mexico (8)
17 Device that operates valves in an internal-combustion engine (8)
19 Having a strong goatish smell (7)
21 Dietary course of treatment (7)
22 Relating to length (6)
25 King of Tyre who supplied Solomon with craftsmen and materials for building the temple (5)

18

ACROSS

1 Author whose works include *The Mousetrap* (6,8)

9 Extremely cold and icy spell of weather (6-2)

10 Proprietor of possessor (5)

12 River flowing into North Sea at Hamburg (4)

13 Meat cooked on a skewer (5,5)

15 Of the writing of books (8)

16 Paul —— , American patriot (6)

18 Miserable, pitiful creature (6)

20 Below the ocean (8)

23 Lively Neapolitan dance (10)

24 Large desert in central Asia (4)

26 Recess in a wall (5)

27 Engrave or etch (8)

28 Wine bottle holding equivalent of 20 normal bottles (14)

DOWN

2 Performer of spectacular gymnastic feats (7)

3 Back part of the foot (4)

4 This cat grinned in *Alice's Adventures in Wonderland* (8)

5 Meal or the food supplied at a meal (6)

6 Grocer or butcher perhaps (10)

7 Dishonourable, of low birth (7)

8 Questionable or uncertain (11)

11 Largest national park in USA (mostly in NW Wyoming) (11)

14 Cushion-shaped piece of veal (10)

17 Broken down and examined critically (8)

19 More common name for otalgia (7)

21 Business of entertaining (7)

22 Object to which one is irrationally devoted (6)

25 Soft French cheese (4)

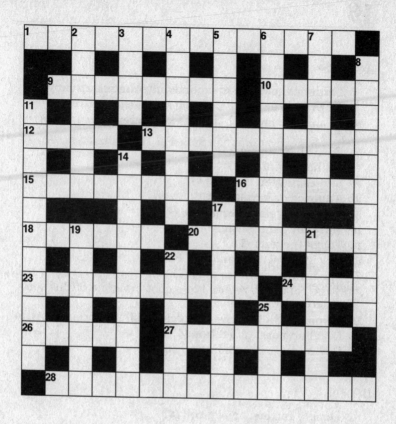

ACROSS

1 Large snake that coils round and squeezes its prey **(11)**
9 Word used by Scots meaning strange or unusual **(4)**
10 Of an instrument that measures differences in hearing **(11)**
11 Eastern European **(4)**
14 Author of *Lolita* **(7)**
16 Largest city in Israel **(3,4)**
17 Annoyed or irritated **(5)**
18 Type of vegetable eg potato **(4)**
19 Novel by Jane Austen **(4)**
20 Top of the milk **(5)**
22 Disciple and companion of Paul **(7)**
23 Theoretical, in name only **(7)**
24 Swiss folk hero reputed to a shot an apple off his son's head **(4)**
28 Whole body of believers in Jesus **(11)**
29 Legal or moral obligation **(4)**
30 Deviousness in avoiding straightforward action **(11)**

DOWN

2 Female gamete, an egg-cell **(4)**
3 Flashy black-marketeer **(4)**
4 Dynasty that ruled Russia from **1613-1917 (7)**
5 Shelter for doves and pigeons **(4)**
6 Left out, failed to do something **(7)**
7 The act of subjugating to a dominating influence **(11)**
8 In a sociable or cheerful way **(10)**
12 Lack of thanks **(11)**
13 Something that is different from what is expected or usual **(11)**
15 Tawny thrush of North America **(5)**
16 American from a southern state **(5)**
20 Russian dramatist, author of *The Cherry Orchard* **(7)**
21 This cocktail is an incendiary bomb **(7)**
25 Norfolk town near Suffolk border **(4)**
26 Of unknown authorship **(4)**
27 Non-flowering plant growing in dense mats **(4)**

ACROSS

1 Wooded highland region in Germany (5,6)
8 Reddish cactus of the genus Opuntia (7-4)
11 Onion-like vegetable that is an emblem of Wales (4)
12 Chinese guild or secret society (4)
13 Of the wind, changing direction clockwise (7)
15 Rotating aerial (7)
16 Plant of the heath genus (5)
17 Diana —— , lead singer with the group the *Supremes* (4)
18 British general in World War I who became Governor-General of Canada 1921-6 (4)
19 Public, open to view (5)
21 Marsupial smaller than the kangaroo (7)
22 State of agitation or excitement (7)
23 Woman's loose undergarment (4)
26 Standard unit of currency in some Central and South American countries (4)
27 Herbivorous dinosaur (11)
28 Relating to jazz style originating in New Orleans (11)

DOWN

2 Keep out of sight and lie in wait (4)
3 Alkaloid drug which is potentially hallucinogenic (7)
4 Music which often evokes the events of daily life (4)
5 Exact copy often on a smaller scale (7)
6 Trivial or slight fight or quarrel (4)
7 Dickens character who wanted more (6,5)
8 He plays Norman Clegg in *Last of the Summer Wine* (5,6)
9 Co-star in *The Likely Lads* (6,5)
10 The act or process of combining together (11)
14 Juices released by meat while it is cooking (5)
15 Flaking or peeling substance such as dandruff (5)
19 Constrained or gratified (7)
20 Wheeled shelter used by Roman besiegers (7)
24 Prefix denoting feather or wing (4)
25 Interjection to draw one's attention quietly (4)
26 Feline also known as the cougar (4)

ACROSS

1 South Africa's largest city (12)
8 Small monkey similar to the marmoset (7)
9 Belgium's chief port (7)
11 Arranged according to plan (4,3)
12 Having a more stippled effect (7)
13 Fill with high spirits (5)
14 Scottish city in 20 region (9)
16 Jesus's birthplace (9)
19 Pronounced with the back of the tongue (5)
21 Room or place of total privacy (7)
23 Italian rice dish (7)
24 One plucking a musical instrument perhaps (7)
25 Being more irritating (7)
26 Judicial capital of South Africa (12)

DOWN

1 Kingston is the capital of this West Indian island (7)
2 Regulatory substance produced in the body (7)
3 Last hole of 5th round of golf? (9)
4 South African antelope (5)
5 Vessel used for washing oneself all over (7)
6 More shrill or piping (7)
7 40 km from Cape Town, the second oldest city in South Africa (12)
10 Seaport capital of Rivers State in southern Nigeria (4,8)
15 Form of baptism involving whole or partial submerging of a person's body in water (9)
17 Plant's coiling threadlike climbing organ (8)
18 Network of crossed bars (7)
19 Sac containing serous fluid (7)
20 14 area of Scotland (7)
22 Central or repeated theme (5)

ACROSS

1 Winged horse said to have sprung from Medusa's blood (7)
5 Pouched-billed water-fowl (7)
9 Two crotchets or half a semibreve (5)
10 Old record-player (9)
11 Science of computing time (10)
12 William —— the Elder, 1st Earl of Chatham (4)
14 Carousel, a fairground attraction (5-2-5)
18 Adam and Eve's home (6,2,4)
21 Having a distinctively lively and spirited quality (4)
22 Impaired validity of claim (10)
25 European bird fond of eating thistle seeds (9)
26 First of the choice of calls a team captain might make (5)
27 Go back over one's steps again (7)
28 Certificate of qualification (7)

DOWN

1 Volcanic rock used for scouring (6)
2 Bridge-like framework over railway lines (6)
3 Disciple known as the *Rock* (5,5)
4 Pertaining to the calf of the leg (5)
5 Dogmatic teacher (9)
6 Vientiane is the capital of this Asian country (4)
7 Intricate ornamental twist (8)
8 Unsegmented worm (8)
13 Amicable feeling towards others (10)
15 River forming border between USA and Mexico (3,6)
16 Jelly prepared from seaweed (4-4)
17 Ornamental chain worn round the wrist (8)
19 Having eight lines to the sheet (6)
20 Black Sea port in S Ukraine (6)
23 Holy war (Muslim) (5)
24 King of Mercia 757-796, dyke builder (4)

23

ACROSS

1 Jerusalem garden where Jesus was betrayed on the night before his Crucifixion (10)
6 Short tail of a deer or rabbit (4)
9 String-operated puppet (10)
10 Author of the *Book of Nonsense* (4)
12 Extreme folly, utter foolishness (6)
13 Long riding breeches (8)
15 Garden pink with bearded petals (5-7)
18 Formally rebuking severely (12)
21 Small long-tailed parrot (8)
22 Rushing sound of something large passing through the air (6)
24 *The Forsyte* —— , (John Galsworthy) (4)
25 Vendor of household hardware (10)
26 Run with long strides (4)
27 Not refined or genteel (10)

DOWN

1 Take risks, play for money (6)
2 Omagh is the county town of this Northern Ireland county (6)
3 Spirit distilled North of the Border (6,6)
4 Literary manner or bearing (4)
5 Covering the whole country (10)
7 Celestial chubby-faced winged children (8)
8 Tedious, annoying or troublesome (8)
11 Charitable regard for fellow human beings (12)
14 Ten-sided figure (10)
16 Offer of marriage (8)
17 Space between electrodes (5-3)
19 Boy in Rudyard Kipling's *The Jungle Book* (6)
20 Supervision of guardianship (6)
23 Obsolete Indian coin (4)

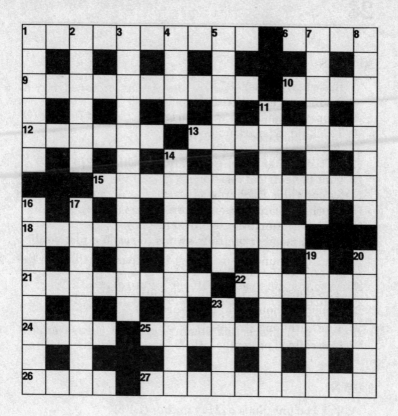

24

ACROSS

1 British SF writer (1,1,5)
5 Swollen inflamed area (7)
9 Tropical plant with waxy, brightly-colouted flowers (7)
10 Thick-furred marsupial (7)
11 Jewelled headdress (5)
12 British writer & politician created CH in 1970 (1,1,7)
13 Unit ofelectrical resistance (7)
14 Its capital is Bucharest (7)
16 South African politician born in 1916 (1,1,5)
19 Desk with flexible cover of slats (4-3)
22 Female member of group sworn to reach a just verdict in court (9)
24 Ahead; at an advantage (3-2)
25 Examination to ascertain one's state of health (7)
26 Whirling sensation when balance is disturbed (7)
27 Person of importance? (7)
28 Action of spacecraft coming into the earth's atmosphere (2-5)

DOWN

1 *The Darling Buds of May author* (1,1,5)
2 Gloucestershire & England cricketer (1848-1915) (1,1,5)
3 Distinguishing mark of the face (9)
4 Percoid marine fish (3-4)
5 Unnamed team member (1,1,5)
6 River (with Avon) flowing into the English channel at Christchurch (5)
7 Towards the Orient (7)
8 Mountainous West Indonesian island (7)
15 State capital of Victoria (9)
16 British detective novelist (1,1,5)
17 Tedium, ennui (7)
18 *Winnie the Pooh* author (1,1,5)
19 Knock down with a moving vehicle (3,4)
20 British poet, dramatist & critic born in the US (1,1,5)
21 Singer of the 1964 hit *Hold Me* (1,1,5)
23 Mad or eccentric (5)

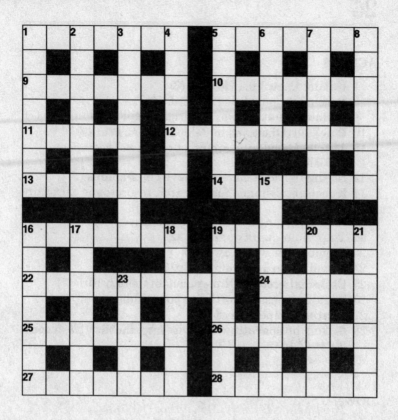

ACROSS

1 Hamlet knew him, Horatio (**6**)
4 **N**ine might be bowled at Lords (**8**)
9 Follower of **4** who was Chairman (**6**)
10 **D**efeated Athenians in Peloponnesian **W**ar (**8**)
12 31 & 26 Pioneering architect of glass skyscrapers (**4,3,3,4**)
13 Mythological shepherdess loved by **D**aphnis (**5**)
14 **N**obel prizewinner for research into atomic structure (**4**)
17 Authority for the nation's lighthouses (**7,5**)
20 The colour quality of light (**12**)
23 Previous king of **N**orway (**4**)
24 Hundred-eyed guardian of Io (**5**)
25 Collected books of **N**orwegian mythology (**4**)
28 Scottish town on **N**orth Sea coast (**8**)
29 Continental ferry port (**6**)
30 **D**uke whose death was devised by Richard III according to Shakespeare (**8**)
31 *See 12*

DOWN

1 Japanese commander in **WW2** (**8**)
2 Erstwhile name of Zimbabwe (**8**)
3 & 8 aka The Mafia (**4,6**)
5 Literally a river-horse! (**12**)
6 Pyromaniacal Emperor? (**4**)
7 Tract of pasture land (**6**)
8 *See 3*
11 Ruling by wealth (**12**)
15 Large bay (**5**)
16 Submarine detection apparatus (**5**)
18 Common name for *Convolvus* plant (**8**)
19 Leading **10** and character in Shakespeare's **D**ream (**8**)
21 Tesseral design (**6**)
22 Its capital city is Lusaka (**6**)
26 *See 12*
27 Largest continent (**4**)

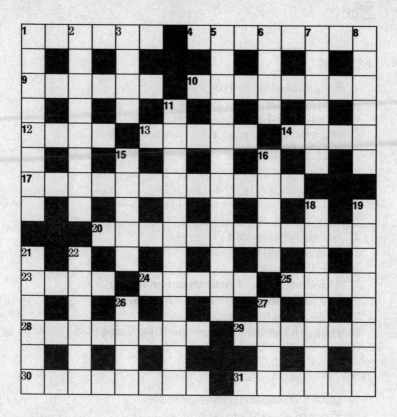

ACROSS

1 US political party (10)
6 Biblical land by the Dead Sea (4)
10 Rouen Cathedral painter! (5)
11 Slaughtered by Herod (9)
12 & 24 Founder of the Jesuits (8,2,6
13 Tribe led by Queen Boudicca (5)
15 Politico-economic doctrine (7)
17 Canadian state with capital Edmonton (7)
19 —— and 22, keyboard composition (7)
21 Knightly splendour (7)
22 Famously with 19 by Widor (5)
24 *See 12*
27 The sharp edge of Arthurian legend! (9)
28 Feudal bond of duty to one's lord (5)
29 Sailing vessel of Arabian Sea (4)
30 Historic English town on the River Lugg (10)

DOWN

1 Late 17th century Parliament (4)
2 Piece of elegant praise (9)
3 Former South African premier (5)
4 Element with atomic number 77 (7)
5 Condition of memory loss (7)
7 Weighty snow-leopard! (5)
8 Beaten on the soles of the feet as torturous punishment (10)
9 Russian composer and pianist (8)
14 Former cattlemarket in London (10)
16 Spanish queen of Castile (8)
18 Call to mind (9)
20 Detectable by ear (7)
21 Bunyan's was able to progress! (7)
23 Type of lizard (5)
25 Large white-flowered Chinese magnolia (5)
26 Shakespearean monarch (4)

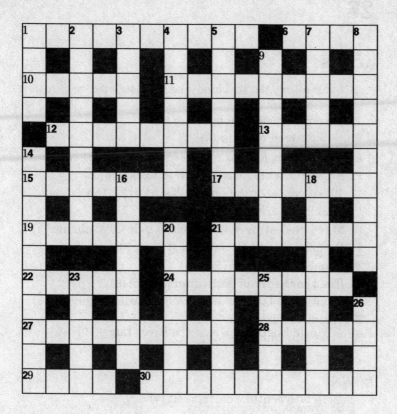

ACROSS

8 Lack of oxygen in blood due to restricted respiration (8)

9 Extension to a main building (6)

10 —— Steiger, filmstar (3)

11 Figure formed by two intersecting planes (8)

12 SF writer & biochemist born in Russia (6)

13 TV sit-com starring Pauline Quirke (5,2,1,7)

15 Recklessly drive a stolen car (3-4)

18 Machine-destroyer, opponent of industrial change (7)

21 Resort on north Norfolk coast (5-4-3-3)

24 Panacea or cure-all (6)

25 Plant of the genus *Delphinium* (8)

26 International language developed from Esperanto (3)

27 Weedy rye-grass (6)

28 Possessing aptitude (8)

DOWN

1 St Francis' birthplace (6)

2 Broad plate carried for deflecting weapons (6)

3 In a remarkable way (15)

4 Surrey town south west of Aldershot (7)

5 Opera by Puccini (6,9)

6 Consecrated with oil (8)

7 One who interprets or explains (8)

14 Flat-bodied fish, eg skate (3)

16 On the next page (8)

17 Substance having the effect of slackening or making less severe (8)

19 Possessive pronoun (3)

20 Aquatic Mexican salamander (7)

22 One of a small fraternity of ascetic Jews (6)

23 Sweated or oozed out (6)

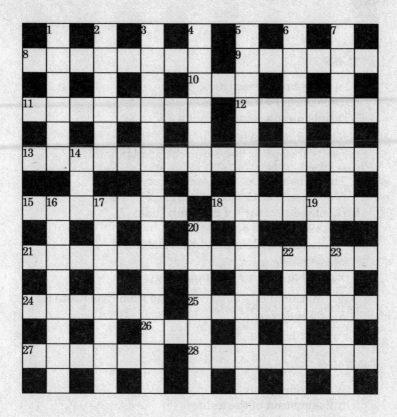

28

ACROSS

  1 A venereal disease (10)
  6 Type of rugby forward (4)
10 A lightweight motorcycle (5)
11 Native of a region of northern Scandinavia (9)
12 Part of the church at right angles to the nave (8)
13 A Greek order of architecture (5)
15 Turkish empire of the 14th century (7)
17 A peninsula of Central America (7)
19 Disputed territory of northern India (7)
21 The fastest land animal (7)
22 "Well done" (when said to a female) (5)
24 Shackles (8)
27 The office of a Jewish leader (9)
28 The fist (5)
29 The —— of the Apostles (4)
30 Five-faced solid figures (10)

DOWN

  1 Wild animals hunted for sport (4)
  2 Inflammation of the kidneys (9)
  3 French sculptor (5)
  4 German artist who was appointed painter to Henry VIII (7)
  5 Full appreciation of another's feelings (7)
  7 The use of radio impulses for locating objects (5)
  8 Thorny evergreen shrub related to hawthorn (10)
  9 Member of a Jewish priestly sect opposed to the Pharisees (8)
14 An Australian kingfisher (10)
16 Class of animals that suckle their young (8)
18 Document which proves the right to possession (5,4)
20 Storm about (7)
21 Competition (7)
23 Male head of a religious institution (5)
25 Shell used as a trumpet (5)
26 Flat-topped hill with steep sides (4)

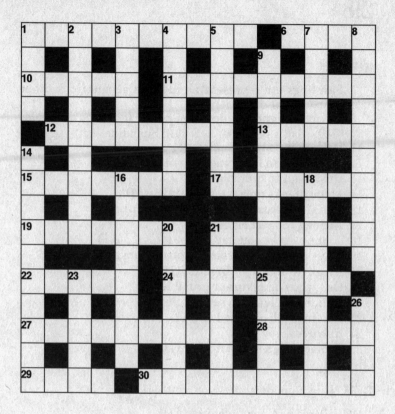

29

ACROSS

1 Paintings etc representing ideas in geometric & other designs (8,3)
8 Promise that often does not occur (as Alice was told) (3,8)
11 Behave sulkily, be listless (4)
12 West African instrument similar to the harp (4)
13 Dusty, apt to crumble (7)
15 Made planks on a boat watertight (7)
16 Ned —— , Australian folk-figure (5)
17 Africa's longest river (4)
18 Johnny —— , country singer (4)
19 River that flows through Nottingham and Stoke (5)
21 Essex resort NE of Clacton (7)
22 One who complains or grumbles (7)
23 Italian city built on seven hills (4)
26 Roofing slab of baked clay (4)
27 Revolving toy (8,3)
28 Zodiacal sign of the Archer (11)

DOWN

2 Hillside or slope in Scotland (4)
3 Meadow pipit (7)
4 Egyptian dancing-girl (4)
5 Resort adjoining Paignton (7)
6 Crow-like bird (4)
7 Comic opera by Gilbert and Sullivan (1,1,1,8)
8 Rugby union full-back who played 55 times for Wales (1,1,1,8)
9 Refinement of finish of completed product (11)
10 Professional cheat or swindler (4-7)
14 Have an intense desire or longing (5)
15 ——-film, used to wrap food etc (5)
19 City in the Hainaut province of Belgium (7)
20 Lever used to fire a gun (7)
24 Hebrew measure of about a bushel (4)
25 Part of the Highland dress (4)

26 Soya-bean curd (4)

30

ACROSS

1 Canal-building Duke (11)
10 Suggest (5)
11 Cutting marine creature? (9)
12 Action of reckless daring (7-2)
13 God of the mid-week (5)
14 German Army commander nicknamed The Desert Fox (6)
16 Italian artist court-painter to Charles II of Spain (8)
18 Sobriquet of Wellington (4,4)
20 Of poets like Shakespeare (6)
23 Computer tycoon Alan who won his spurs! (5)
24 Leading academic who once won the Cheltenham Gold Cup! (3,6)
26 Balletic leap with touching heels (9)
27 Last state of insect life (5)
28 Female pop singer had a big hit with *All Cried Out* (6,5)

DOWN

2 Surname of Thomas More's biographer and son-in-law (5)
3 Period characterised by light (7)
4 Lowest commissioned officer rank in British infantry (6)
5 Written defence or vindication (8)
6 One settling a permanent provision on someone or body (7)
7 Midlands harrier town (13)
8 Islands in the Caribbean (8)
9 Reference to Macbeth by the witches (5,2,6)
15 Part of the City of London where tube-train disaster occurred (8)
17 Those by Boz were the serialised writings of Charles Dickens (8)
19 Author of *The Alexandria Quartet* (7)
21 Forename of explorer Vespucci giving name to present USA (7)
22 Photographer to nobility and the rich (6)
25 Contractual conditions of letting (5)

31

ACROSS

1 Former name of Vanuatu, a group of islands west of Fiji (3,8)

7 One of a number of flat rings of iron or plastic used in a game of the same name (5)

8 Slip used in the game of spillikins (4-5)

10 Expression of regret for doing wrong (7)

11 Famous street in Edinburgh (7)

12 Dicken's Oliver (5)

13 Cyclically returning pattern for the living things (9)

16 Characterised by periods of diminished severity (9)

18 Egyptian ram-headed god (5)

19 The largest breed of penguin (7)

22 Edible entrails in a cooked loaf (alternative spelling) (7)

23 Novel by R L Stevenson (9)

24 Pickled flower-bud used as a condiment (5)

25 Adventure story by John Buchan (11)

DOWN

1 Newly-coined word or phrase (9)

2 Archaic word for outside (7)

3 Giving pleasure, delightful (9)

4 Go over the main points again (5)

5 Unit of two lines making a couplet (7)

6 Pillar-like formation of glacial ice (5)

7 Part of ship used by cabin passengers and superior officers (7-4)

9 London borough with an abbey and an Roman Catholic cathedral (11)

14 Eight-faced solid plane figures (9)

15 Photography recording a very slow process (4-5)

17 One of a series of horizontal flat areas on a hillside (7)

18 Downy orange-coloured edible fruit (7)

20 Canine without an owner (2-3)

21 North Yorkshire city, arguably England's second oldest town (5)

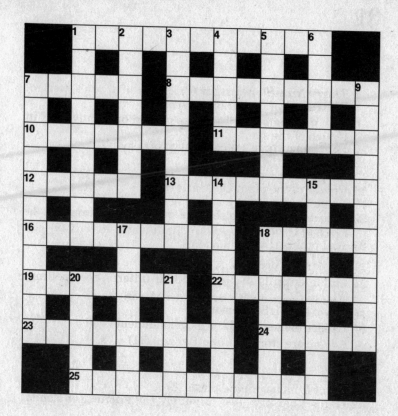

32

ACROSS

1 *Thirty-Nine Steps* author (6)
4 Protrusion of the large intestine (8)
9 & 3 Corrosive substance also known as Aqua Fortis (6,4)
10 Foot supports in equestrianism (8)
12 Autumn in the US (4)
13 Imaginary animal created by Lewis Carroll (5)
14 Colour of the plant Gentian (4)
17 In music, the art of combining melodies (12)
20 Palace built by Wolsey and royal residence until the reign of George II (7,5)
23 And others (Latin) (2,2)
24 See 27
25 Genus of large predatory gull (4)
28 Opera by Mozart (k366) (8)
29 Ancient vessel with two banks oars (6)
30 See 7
31 Greece originally (6)

DOWN

1 Saint & name of nine popes (8)
2 Gaius Valerius —— , arguably the greatest of Roman lyric poets (8)
3 See 9
5 Cathedral city and column in *The Daily Telegraph* (12)
6 —— Pound, poet (4)
7 & 30 Naughty ambiguity (6,8)
8 Surgical instrument for scraping bones (6)
11 Business type who sets up a venture usually with his own money (12)
15 Public opinion polls first reported in 1824 (5)
16 Centre of pilgrimage in County Mayo (5)
18 Barry —— , conductor and horn virtuoso (8)
19 Racehorses whose odds shorten dramatically towards the start (8)
21 Formerly British Honduras (6)
22 Seasoned stew of meat & vegetables (6)
26 William —— , founder of one of the Eastern states of the US (4)
27 & 24 Contemporary British playwright & director once married to Alison Steadman (4,5)

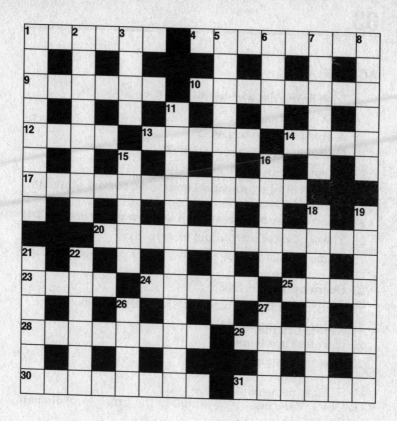

33

ACROSS

4 Irish dramatist who wrote *The Rivals* (8)

8 A skin allergy (6)

9 A breed of large terrier (8)

10 Cross-bearer in a procession (8)

11 A type of delivery in cricket (6)

12 Method of film projection on a wide, curved screen giving a 3-D effect (8)

13 Least distance between high and low water marks (4,4)

16 The science of matter and motion (8)

19 Prime Minister who came to power on May 4th, 1979 (8)

21 Skewer (6)

23 Inadequate flow of blood to a part of the body (8)

24 A flimsy thong sandal (4-4)

25 Jewelled headband (6)

26 Divergent squints (4-4)

DOWN

1 Constellation between Libra and Sagittarius (7)

2 Cancerous blood disease (9)

3 Palm leaf-bast used for weaving (6)

4 The US flag (5,3,7)

5 From an ancient state in Italy, north of the Tiber (8)

6 The sub-continent (5)

7 A weed of the flax family, genus *Radiola* (7)

14 The author of *Vanity Fair* (9)

15 Fine, white kaolin used for earthenware (8)

17 The skullcap worn by Jewish males (7)

18 Measure used to express a level of sound (7)

20 District in Greece whose people lived a simple, rural life (6)

22 Small container for a hyperdermic dose (5)

34

ACROSS

1 Africa's highest peak (11)
7 eg Antler-moth, ie one that comes out at night (7)
8 Gliding dance in duple time (3-4)
10 Archaic word for fidelity or faith (5)
11 Fall-guy, one who takes the blame (9)
12 Second largest city in Iran (7)
14 Greek who drowned in the Hellespont (7)
15 Imaginary mischievous agency (7)
18 Cocktail of brandy, Cointreau and lemon juice (7)
20 Community of organisms and their environment (9)
21 Open fabric used for upholstery etc (5)
22 Dutch philosopher whose main work was *Ethics* (7)
23 Lockjaw (7)
24 Recently televised George Eliot novel (11)

DOWN

1 Start of a football match (4-3)
2 County in Leinster (5)
3 Fourth president of the USA (7)
4 Game played by two teams of seven players (7)
5 Mentioned previously (9)
6 Vended in greater numbers (7)
7 Non-existence (11)
9 Opera by Britten (5,6)
13 Place synonymous with the US film industry (9)
16 Self-conceit (7)
17 Abnormal growth produced by a wasp, usually on an oak-tree (7)
18 Indication of a disease (7)
19 Ancient city in Greece (7)
21 Woodland deity (5)

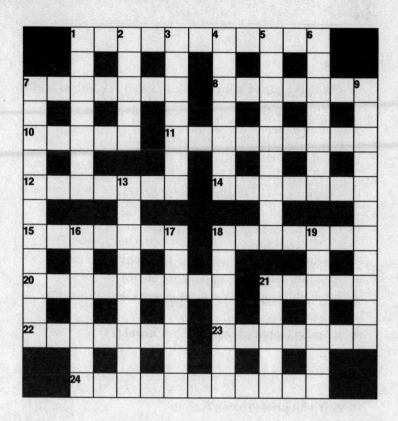

35

ACROSS

1 Biblical King of Babylon who sacked Jerusalem 586BC (14)

9 Slow Spanish dance (8)

10 Constituent of the atmosphere (5)

12 Saint associated with fire at sea! (4)

13 Solid metallic plate for printing...fixed character! (10)

15 Charles —— , French singer of *She* (8)

16 Extremity of connecting rod in engine (3,3)

18 Upper position in the feudal hierarchy (6)

20 Living matter (8)

23 Bellows-powered musical instruments (10)

24 Sparkling Italian white wine (4)

26 Daphnis's beloved shepherdess (5)

27 Place to soak up the sun (8)

28 Now called Istanbul (14)

DOWN

2 A Hindu priest caste (7)

3 African republic (4)

4 Prickly-leaved plant portrayed on Corinthian columns (8)

5 Lowest points (6)

6 Gardens for animals etc (10)

7 Medicine for allaying pain (7)

8 The art of the juggler (11)

11 New birth of art (11)

14 Trees etc permanently in leaf (10)

17 Band worn on the forehead (8)

19 Florentine painter of early 11 into perspective (7)

21 Engrave (in Shakespeare) (7)

22 Holiday or car (6)

25 Measurement of landed herrings (4)

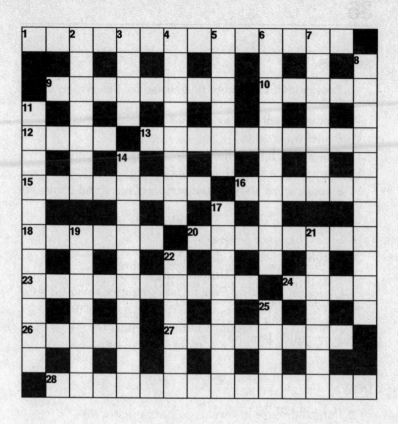

36

ACROSS

1 Eponymous character in a book by Sir Walter Scott (11)

10 Second brightest star in constellation Perseus (5)

11 Bridal wear (9)

12 One with a light & delicate build (9)

13 Nocturnal, arboreal, Madagascan primate (5)

14 Slender spire above intersection of nave and transepts (6)

16 Tall stick to support climbing plants (8)

18 Strict, harsh or severe (8)

20 Edible snail-shaped shellfish (6)

23 One country of the United Kingdom (5)

24 Omission resulting from failure to notice something (9)

26 Association of business enterprises, a cartel (9)

27 Albrecht ——— , German painter & engraver (5)

28 Eponymous hero of a book by George Eliot (5,6)

DOWN

2 Fungal disease in cereals & other grasses (5)

3 Leap about clumsily or joyfully (7)

4 Rising trend or improvement (6)

5 Pulley-like structure through which a tendon passes (8)

6 Fifth letter of the Greek alphabet (7)

7 Town in Pembrokeshire (13)

8 Co-operation, pulling together (8)

9 Canary Island south-west of Lanzarote (13)

15 Aubergine (3-5)

17 Machines imitating living creatures' movements (8)

19 Composer of *The Barber of Seville* (7)

21 Person with access to exclusive information (7)

22 Recover possession (6)

25 Furze (5)

37

ACROSS

1 Novel of the Russian revolution by Boris Pasternak (2,7)
9 Insect with a loud chirping sound (6)
10 Female baptismal sponsor (9)
11 Another name for the Australian wattle (6)
12 Variety of peach with a smooth skin (9)
13 Feeling of disgust or revulsion (6)
17 Exclamation expressing surprise or triumph (3)
19 Novel by Daphne du Maurier (10,5)
20 Look closely or curiously (3)
21 Inexperienced recruit (6)
25 The world's second largest island (discounting Australia) (9)
26 Scottish meat-plates (6)
27 17th century pirate in the West Indies mainly preying on Spanish galleons (9)
28 Less common word meaning come ashore (6)
29 Heroine in *Othello* (9)

DOWN

2 Largest of the Dodecanese Islands in Greece (6)
3 North African supposedly descended from one of Noah's sons (6)
4 Devoted worshipper or adherent (6)
5 French liqueur made from aromatic herbs and flowers (5,10)
6 Stroke of bad luck (9)
7 English royal house (1399-1461) (9)
8 Stringed Russian instrument (9)
14 Forced, with sudden emphasis (mus.) (9)
15 One who dislikes foreigners (9)
16 Book of sacred writings (9)
17 The basic SI unit of electric current (3)
18 An unspecified quantity (3)
22 Took part in sport using swords (6)
23 Fully attended meeting of a legislative body (6)
24 Passage presented to students for translation (6)

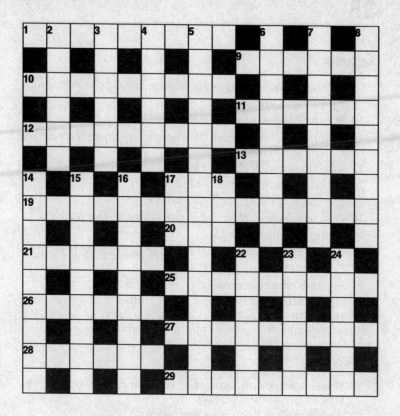

38

ACROSS

1 British novelist and critic known as Q (7-5)
8 Kriss ——, athlete (7)
9 Word of opposite meaning (7)
11 Domination by those in charge or those employing others in US politics (7)
12 Pop singer with the hit *Goody Two Shoes* in 1982 (4,3)
13 Nasal or instrumental sound (5)
14 Acrobats walk or perform on it (9)
16 One who makes charitable donations to the poor (9)
19 Heavy wooden shoe (5)
21 Ceremonial emblems and robes of high office (7)
23 Completely finished (3,4)
24 —— and dearest are one's closest kin (7)
25 Upper arm bone (7)
26 Harrisburg is the capital of this state (12)

DOWN

1 Bitter compound extracted from bark & wood of the tree of the same name (7)
2 Accustoming, becoming hardened to (7)
3 Often repeated theme in a literary work (9)
4 Lariat or lasso (5)
5 One who has been rejected by society (7)
6 Monetary unit of some South & Central American countries and Portugal (7)
7 Series of interconnecting tunnels (6-6)
10 Agnes Gonxha Bojaxuiu, Indian Roman Catholic missionary (6,6)
15 He became General Secretary of the Soviet Communist Party in 1985 (9)
17 Person of power, especially in industry (7)
18 Large sailing ship with at least three masts (7)
19 Son of David and Bathsheba in the OT (7)
20 German state with Munich as capital (7)
22 Appropriately or fittingly (5)

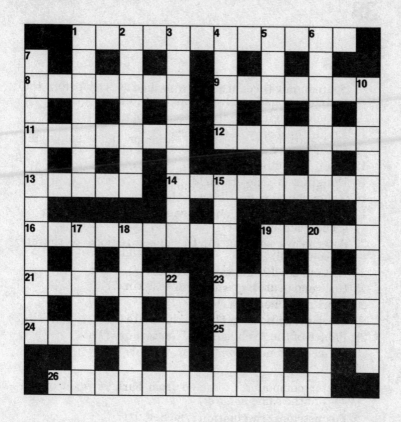

39

ACROSS

1 Spanish naval commander who died shortly before the Spanish Armada sailed to England (5,4)

9 Articles originating from foreign countries (7)

10 Enduring energy or resilience (7)

11 Coarse jute fabric used for bags and upholstery (7)

12 Illicit bar selling alcohol (9)

14 Daughter of a sovereign (8)

15 Yellowish flax, *fine linen* in the Bible (6)

17 Greek mathematician, astonomer and geographer of second century AD (7)

20 Alternative spelling for the upper regions of the atmosphere (6)

23 Long hooded cloak worn by Arabs (8)

25 It's worn to soak up sweat (9)

26 Card game based on rummy (7)

27 Sleep inducing song (7)

28 Palace of the Archbishop of Canterbury (7)

29 Officers attendant on the royal family (9)

DOWN

2 Postmortem examination (7)

3 Male domestic felines (7)

4 One paddlinga small boat (8)

5 Soft or gentle breeze (6)

6 Hereford & Worcester town north-east of Monmouth (4-2-3)

7 Ermine in winter coat (7)

8 British athlete who first ran *the four-minute mile* (9)

13 Book to help one write words correctly (7)

15 Hebridean isle between North and South Uist (9)

16 Fit furniture with padding, springs, coverings etc (9)

18 Lady skilled in muscle treatment (8)

19 —— Moses, US primitive painter (7)

21 —— bells, an orchestral percussion instrument (7)

22 Elevate to the peerage (7)

24 Bandage a limb or wound completely (6)

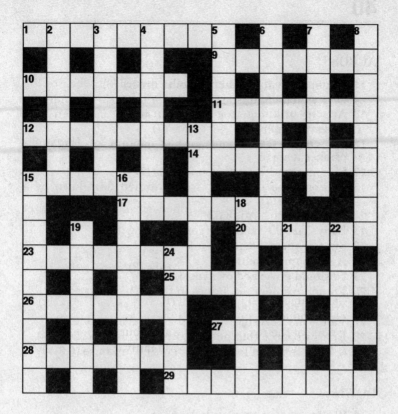

40

ACROSS

1 Angel of the highest of the nine orders (6)

4 City which bid unsuccessfully for the 2000 Olympics (8)

10 Arc of the equator between place meridian and Greenwich (9)

11 TV commentator and former captain of England's cricket team (5)

12 Silk material with woven figures (7)

13 A broad one is a long swallow-tailed flag flown by a commodore (7)

14 The queen to a rajah (5)

15 Lady Thatcher's former constituency (8)

18 Subterranean cemetery (8)

20 A mechanical man (5)

23 National governed by ayatollahs (7)

25 French residence of Popes in the 14th century (7)

26 West African baboon (5)

27 Valentina Tereshkova was the first female one (9)

28 Energy source that never closed during WW2! (8)

29 & **22** Reinforced feature of a church or house (6,6)

DOWN

1 Wolfgang Mozart's birthplace (8)

2 Capital of Burma (7)

3 The Botticelli painting also known *as The Allegory of Spring* (9)

5 Walt Disney classic with music by Tchaikovsky (8,6)

6 Inert gas of the air (5)

7 The International —— fought against Franco (7)

8 Play smoothly without a break between notes (mus.) (6)

9 Husband of *King Lear*'s daughter Regan (4,2,8)

16 Non-meat-eating animal (9)

17 One of London's airports (8)

19 Type of horse or camel (7)

21 French artist and lithographer who founded the Intimist movement (7)

22 *See 29*

24 Religion of country of 23 (5)

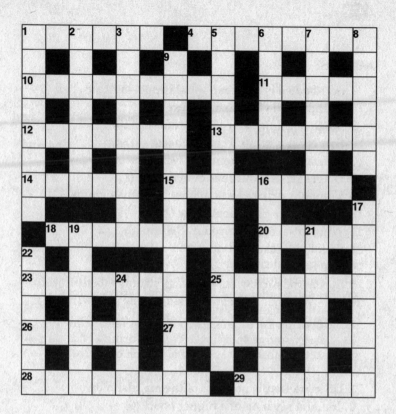

41

ACROSS

1 Soft-bodied crustacean inhabiting a mollusc shell (6-4)
6 Brandy made from fruit-refuse (4)
9 Mode of thinking or understanding (10)
10 Soft creamy white French cheese (4)
12 Freezing compartment of a refrigerator (6)
13 Diagrammatic outlines or synopses (8)
15 Valuable stringed instrument, usually a violin (12)
18 Spectacular theatrical show (12)
21 Wind often experienced in Britain (8)
22 Small pleasure-boat operated with the feet (6)
24 The Eternal City (4)
25 Species of yarrow once used as a snuff substitute (10)
26 —— Williams, US country singer and songwriter (4)
27 Country in West Africa, mainly in the Sahara (10)

DOWN

1 US state that is not part of the mainland (6)
2 Judicial revision of a higher court (6)
3 Part of Kent separated from the mainland by two branches of the river Stour (4,2,6)
4 Thin, flexible stem used for chair seats etc (4)
5 Disappointing conclusion after high expectations (10)
7 Sea east of Italy (8)
8 Deep crack in a glacier (8)
11 An overpowering by strong light (12)
14 1942 film starring Bogart and Bergman (10)
16 Town in Warwickshire near Nuneaton (8)
17 In Greek tragedy, ode sung after chorus had taken their places (8)
19 Monkey with long muzzle and large teeth (6)
20 Heroine of *The Merchant of Venice* (6)
23 River rising in north west County Durham and flowing into the North Sea at Sunderland (4)

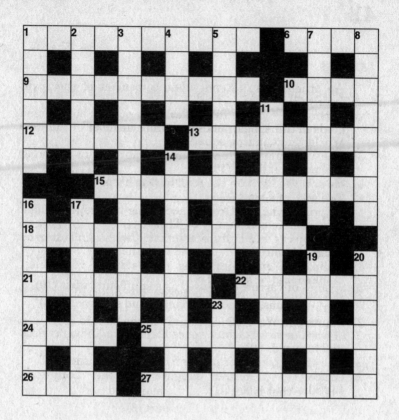

42

ACROSS

7 An official who attends upon a member of the royal family (7)

8 Jimmy —— , the footballer who scored 357 league goals in 517 appearances and was a member of the 1966 World Cup winning squad (7)

10 The minimum illumination required for moving motorcars at night (10)

11 He saw the light on the road to Damascus (4)

12 The wall of a fruit (8)

14 Region of ancient Greece, according to legend, welded into a single community by Theseus (6)

15 The objects and culture associated with mind-altering drugs (11)

19 A Spanish dish containing rice, saffron, vegetables, chicken and/or seafood (6)

20 Belonging to a period between the Silurian and the Carboniferous (8)

22 Brownish purple (4)

23 A word or words which reads the same both backwards and forwards (10)

25 The official enforcer of a university's regulations (7)

26 Grace ——, heroic daughter of the Longstone Lighthouse keeper (7)

DOWN

1 Water-bearing rock (7)

2 A member of the nation which fused with the Persians around 500 BC (4)

3 The name given to Beethoven's third Symphony (6)

4 Horse deportment training (8)

5 —— Mountains, located on the borders of Poland, Rumania and the Ukraine (10)

6 Wart usually found on the sole of the foot (7)

9 English furniture designer 1718-1779 (11)

13 Bankruptcy (10)

16 The jockey who won the 1981 Grand National on Aldaniti (8)

17 First month of the Gregorian calendar which takes its name from the Roman god of gates and doorways (7)

18 An organ named after its inventor, a US mechanical engineer (7)

21 A member of a NE Germanic people who overran Gaul, Spain and sacked Rome (6)
24 A very small brook (4)

43

ACROSS

7 Britain's WW2 prime minister (9)
8 Sir James ——, the Scottish chemist who invented the vacuum flask (5)
10 "Space, the final ——" according to *Star Trek*'s Captain Kirk (8)
11 A squared or dressed stone used in building or facing a wall (6)
12 Large loose hood worn by a monk (4)
13 A well in which water rises up a borehole by hydrostatic pressure from a basin at a higher level (8)
15 According to Greek mythology she opened the box holding all the ills of mankind (7)
17 A Russian country-dance (7)
20 The learned (8)
22 Cricket international (4)
25 The 12th US president (6)
26 The seed capsules of plants of the ginger family used as a spice (8)
27 House made of sun-dried bricks (5)
28 Jazz singer and wife of musician John Dankworth (4,5)

DOWN

1 The English Labour politician who was shadow leader of the Commons 1983-87 (5)
2 The dictator who ruled Spain until his death in 1975 (6)
3 Dick Francis is an exponent of this genre (8)
4 In Latin mottos it means "may it flourish" (7)
5 A healing pool at Jerusalem (8)
6 A Russian guitar-like instrument (9)
9 Hypocritically pious language (4)
14 The Italian patriot who led the 1,000 Red Shirts in the unification of Italy (9)
16 An Arab cloak with a hood and wide sleeves (8)
18 The organisation linking national crime-fighting forces (8)
19 —— green, a bright green cloth which takes its name from the English city where it was first made (7)
21 The location of the Taj Mahal (4)
23 The sacred beetle of ancient Egypt (6)
24 A town of East Lancashire, near to and often linked with Nelson (5)

44

ACROSS

7 A brand of aromatic bitters (9)

8 Actors words direct to the audience (5)

10 Margaret Thatcher's title (8)

11 English egyptologist who discovered Tutankhamen's tomb (6)

12 Labiate garden herb used in cooking (4)

13 Ancient state between Salerno and the Tiber, famous for its art (8)

15 Tungsten (7)

17 Fat from wool (7)

20 A ball of perfumes (8)

22 One name for the Earth-mother in Assyro-Babylonian mythology (4)

25 Bird of prey that's trained to pursue game (6)

26 Terrestrial squirrel of North America (8)

27 Mel —— , singer born in Illinois, 1925 (5)

28 A statue of Pallas on which the safety of Troy depended (9)

DOWN

1 "Slamming Sam", US golfer holding a record number of US Tour wins (84) (5)

2 A coloured ring round the sun or moon (6)

3 Island in the South Atlantic where Napoleon was exiled (2,6)

4 German city virtually destroyed by bombing in WW2 (7)

5 Type of coffee making machine (8)

6 Hormone which raises the blood pressure (9)

9 Maple genus (4)

14 1992 Olympic men's high jump champion (9)

16 Jockey who was National Hunt champion eight times (8)

18 One of the Leeward Islands (8)

19 States now known as the United Arab Emirates (7)

21 Sand hill (4)

23 Greek letter 'l' (6)

24 Police informer (5)

45

ACROSS

7 Warm, coastal district (7)
8 In French, it's placed under *c* for softness (7)
10 Small dogs named after a place in Mexico (10)
11 Saint of Avalon & Lincoln whose feast-day is November 17 (4)
12 Dry brandy of south west France (8)
14 One of the bridges on the Grand Canal, Venice (6)
15 A psychotic illness, beginning in late childhood, ending in dementia (11)
19 One of the living dead (6)
20 Civility and courteousness (8)
22 Pantheistic Muslim mystic (4)
23 British general who lost the battle for Ticonderoga against the French in Canada, 1758 (10)
25 A mosquito-borne disease (7)
26 Capital of Nicaragua (7)

DOWN

1 One of three English kings (7)
2 One of a Indian monotheistic sect founded by Nanak (4)
3 Admit to holy office (6)
4 Small tiles which make up a mosaic (8)
5 The nationality of President Vytautas Landsbergis (10)
6 Military slang for home (7)
9 Syndrome where real illness is feigned to obtain medical attention (11)
13 Country which had a running war with Armenia (10)
16 The music performed when the host is raised in RC services (8)
17 The river running through Washington DC (7)
18 Antimony (7)
21 Author of *The Thirty-nine Steps* (6)
24 One of three kings of Norway in the 10th and 11th centuries (4)

46

ACROSS

7 The right-hand side of a ship (9)

8 Sculptor whose works included *Le Baiser* and *Le Penseur* (5)

10 A ribbon-shaped, segmented parasite (8)

11 A pale yellow gum resin from the lentisk tree used for varnish, cement etc (6)

12 Those who go to the right in the division lobby (4)

13 First portion of the small intestine (8)

15 The former name of Taiwan (7)

17 An island of the Windward Isles known as *Helen of the West* (2,5)

20 Fighting ship (3-2-3)

22 —— *facto*; the Latin expression meaning "thereby" (4)

25 Elizabeth ——; star of *National Velvet* among other films (6)

26 Capital of 17 (8)

27 Singer and former schoolmaster, born Gordon Sumner in Newcastle in 1951 (5)

28 The sea in which 17 is located (9)

DOWN

1 The northern species of weasel (5)

2 Vessel carrying blood from the heart (6)

3 —— of Rhodes; one of the *Seven Wonders of the World* (8)

4 Sedative for eg soldiers and prisoners (7)

5 The author of *Du Contrat Social* which opens "L'homme est né libre, et partout il est dans les fers." (8)

6 A reddish pigment in bile (9)

9 The boss of a shield (4)

14 Napoleon ——; French emperor (9)

16 TRact of untilled ground often covered with heath (8)

18 Spiral dive of an aeroplane (8)

19 Crosslike (7)

21 An administrative or electoral division of a town (4)

23 Periodically flashing light (6)

24 Covered chair for one carried on two poles (5)

47

ACROSS

1 Wife of Hector in Greek mythology (10)
6 City in W central Russia at confluence of Rivers Irtysh and Om (4)
9 Cut of beef above leg and below aitchbone (10)
10 Thick lump of earth (4)
12 Silk or fine wool scarf worn especially by men under a shirt (6)
13 *See 1 down*
15 Frame for airing laundry (7-5)
18 Energy-producing compound (12)
21 Form of government with a king or queen (8)
22 Disease caused by lack of vitamin C (6)
24 Beardless Himalayan wild goat (4)
25 Outline of a solid figure (10)
26 Pinkish table wine (4)
27 Lower posterior part of the brain (10)

DOWN

1 & 13 Area of NE France under German rule 1871-1919 and 1940-44 (6,8)
2 US city where President Kennedy was assassinated in 1963 (6)
3 Comedy series starring Ronnie Barker and David Jason (4,3,5)
4 Arched recess in a church (4)
5 Science of measurement and analysis of water (10)
7 A thousand million (8)
8 British dish of rice, cooked fish and hard-boiled eggs (8)
11 Art or science of building (12)
14 Very poisonous substance from seeds of *nux vomica* plant (10)
16 Curved oriental sword (8)
17 Fork of the windpipe (8)
19 *Hansel and* ——, fairy-tale (6)
20 Aristotelian school of philosophy (6)
23 Clarified Indian butter (4)

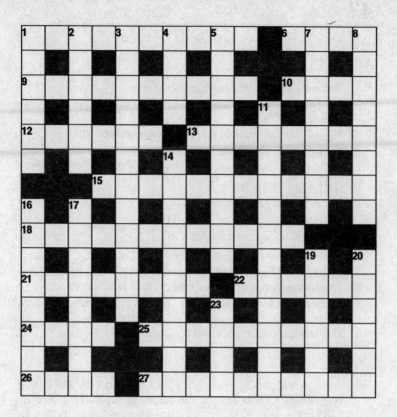

48

ACROSS

1 Detached area off Morocco (4,7)

10 Oranjestad is the capital of this detached area off Venezuela (5)

11 Firm heart-shaped variety of sweet cherry (9)

12 Detached area off Morocco (9)

13 The lowest point, opposite of zenith (5)

14 Drink of the gods (6)

16 Detached area off Morocco (8)

18 Ornamental engraved design (8)

20 Systematic course of action (6)

23 Detached area off North Devon (5)

24 Detached area between Benbecula and Barra... (5,4)

26 ...detached area between Harris and Benbecula (5,4)

27 Agricultural machine used in making bundles of hay (5)

28 Deviation from a particular plane (11)

DOWN

2 N French city, scene of the burning of Joan of Arc in 1431 (5)

3 Waterfalls on US/Canadian border (7)

4 Archaic or poetic name for Britain or England (6)

5 Detached area in North Wales (8)

6 Able to be seen and within striking distance (2,5)

7 Detached area east of Portsmouth (7,6)

8 Phrase at top of newspaper story (8)

9 Detached area off Morocco (13)

15 Curve formed by flexible chain hanging freely between two supports (8)

17 Kitchen waste used as animal feed (8)

19 Fabulous creature with eagle's head and wings and a lion's body (7)

21 Live together as if husband and wife (7)

22 A Muslim ruler (6)

25 Traditional Inuit snow-house (5)

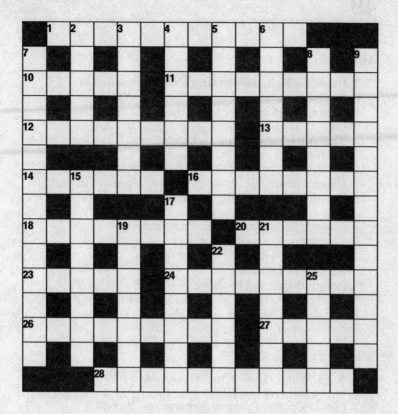

49

ACROSS

1 Plant with clusters of tiny blue flowers (6-2-3)
9 Living both on land and in the water (9)
10 Large forest tree with smooth bark and glossy leaves (5)
11 This horse, according to legend, was filled with armed Greeks (6)
12 Fruit of the tropical Asian palm, the areca (5-3)
13 US composer whose songs include *Swanee River* (6)
15 One who is hypocritical and pretends to be religious (8)
18 Boxer who leads with his right hand (8)
19 Winged heavenly being (6)
21 Putting up without giving in (8)
23 Agitate or incite (4,2)
26 Rough or grating to the senses (5)
27 Alternative Italian plural for bell-towers (9)
28 Another name for woody nightshade (11)

DOWN

1 & 18 When Good King Wenceslas looked out according to the carol (5,2,7)
2 Modern copy of period furniture (abbr.) (5)
3 English queen born in 1533 (9)
4 Frank —— , former regular contestant in *Call My Bluff* (4)
5 Element that's not an alloy (3-5)
6 Article of furniture on trestles perhaps (5)
7 & 20 Cousin of Jesus, a son of Zacharias (4,3,7)
8 & 14 *Absolutely Fabulous* star (8,8)
14 *See 8*
16 Inhabitants from an island in the S Pacific (9)
17 Panelled woodwork (8)
18 *See 1 down*
20 *See 7*
22 Poetic title for Egypt as the dragon as mentioned in Isaiah 51:9 (5)
24 River flowing through Switzerland, Germany and The Netherlands (5)
25 Captain Hook's mate (4)

50

ACROSS

1 Another name for 19 down (12)
8 Branch of mathematics using symbols (7)
9 Painful inflammation of the finger (7)
11 Viscount Nelson's Christian name (7)
12 Work done in harsh conditions for poor pay (7)
13 The lowest point (5)
14 Rest satisfied without raising any objection (9)
16 Sound of the trumpet (9)
19 Painting done on dry plaster (5)
21 A distillation product from coaltar (7)
23 Ask as a favour (7)
24 Pool used for collecting filthy water (7)
25 Jeff ——— , one of the great Australian fast bowlers (7)
26 Actress who plays Pauline Fowler in *Eastenders* (5,7)

DOWN

1 Had a bet (7)
2 Large marine decapod crustacean (7)
3 Woman with whom one is in love (9)
4 Academic robes (5)
5 Japanese art of paper-folding (7)
6 State of bad health (7)
7 Capital of the USA and its location (10,2)
10 Lead singer of *The Mindbenders* pop group (5,7)
15 Involving the square but no higher power in an equation in 8 (9)
17 Answer with a quick return (7)
18 Item of writing material, a memo-block (4-3)
19 Giant Californian redwood tree (7)
20 Wrinkled or folded (7)
22 Surname of first woman to sit in the House of Commons (5)

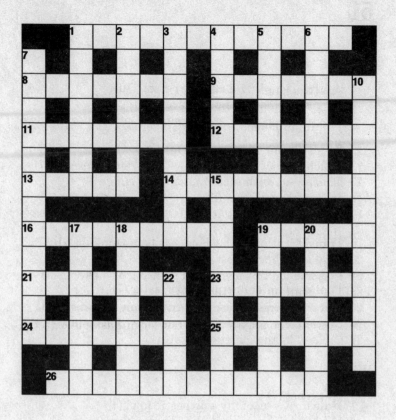

51

ACROSS

1 Informal word for a miserly person (10)
6 Largest island of Inner Hebrides (4)
9 One with fanatical or exaggerated pride in one's own country (10)
10 Endorsement on a passport (4)
13 Vyacheslav Mikhailovich —— , Soviet statesman (7)
15 Isaac —— , author of *Foundation Trilogy* (6)
16 Sticky, chewy sweet (6)
17 North American plant similar to the cuckoo-pint (4-2-3-6)
18 Transliteration of the Japanese name for Japan (6)
20 Seaport in north-west Belgium (6)
21 Do some improvements to a painting or make-up (7)
22 The smallest in a litter of pigs (4)
25 Electric machine used for turning and shaping (5-5)
26 Castlebar is the county town of this Irish county (4)
27 Created by the imagination (10)

DOWN

1 Male bird, especially a domestic fowl (4)
2 Mild Dutch cheese with a red outer skin (4)
3 Ivan Petrovich —— , Russian physiologist (6)
4 Title given to the oak-tree (4,2,3,6)
5 A Henry VIII shilling or later a sixpence (6)
7 War-game that's played on a map for training officers (10)
8 Precision or correctness (10)
11 A burlesque potentate, an imaginary figure of considerable power and self-importance (10)
12 Niggardly person (10)
13 Genus of very large lizards (7)
14 Stylish or fashionable (7)
19 Oil distilled from orange flowers (6)
20 American leopard-like cat (6)
23 Emperor of Holy Roman Empire 962-973AD (4)
24 Chief god of the ancient Greeks (4)

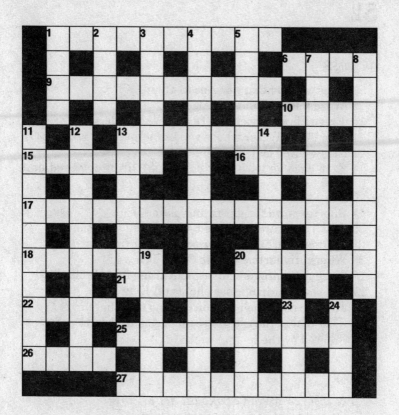

52

ACROSS

1 Type of incendiary device (5-4)
9 Word formed from initials (7)
10 Breed of owl which utters a shrill cry (7)
11 French composer whose works include *Les Troyens* (7)
12 Straw-filled mattress (9)
14 & 15 Female with very pale, light silver-coloured hair (8,6)
15 *See 14*
17 Shorter word for a printing plate (7)
20 Small creature with head, thorax and abdomen (6)
23 N American farm owner or manager (8)
25 Alternative name for the Great Bear (4,5)
26 King of Scotland who became king after Macbeth (7)
27 —— Sands, dangerous shoals off Kent (7)
28 Ken —— , British film director (7)
29 This edible rock is made up of brittle pastel- coloured sticks (9)

DOWN

2 & 15 Presenter of *Strike it Lucky* (7,9)
3 Government of former Soviet Union (7)
4 Type of thick white sauce flavoured with onions and seasoning (8)
5 Freshwater fish of the carp family (6)
6 A proportionate distribution (9)
7 Midwest state south of Lake Michigan (7)
8 Astonishment or wonder (9)
13 Phil —— , US record producer noted for his "wall of sound" (7)
15 *See 2*
16 Removed from king's seat (9)
18 Old light and graceful dance in duple time (8)
19 One skilled in detailed chemical examination (7)
21 Jail where Rudolf Hess was held (7)
22 These towers are hollow structures in which steam is condensed (7)
24 Low rolling noise like thunder (6)

53

ACROSS

1 Naomi James is a lone example of one (11)
7 Brutish creature in *Gulliver's Travels* (5)
8 Consistency, agreement between things (9)
10 Person from an East African republic near Lake Victoria (7)
11 Zoological name for a vertebra (7)
12 Birthmarks or moles (5)
13 Hunchbacked bellringer in Hugo's *Notre-Dame de Paris* (9)
16 Most downy or fleecy (9)
18 Capital of Byelorussia (5)
19 Word having the same sound as another (7)
22 Type of humming-bird (7)
23 Italian or Italian-style restaurant (9)
24 Waterfall slide (5)
25 Persistent, often stupid or idle talk (7-4)

DOWN

1 Sailors' chant whilst hauling on ropes (2-5-2)
2 Another word for cartilages (7)
3 Proficiency or refinement in artistic performance (9)
4 Currents of air (5)
5 Italian wireless pioneer (7)
6 River or spring nymph (5)
7 Something that's unspecified but well-understood (3-4-4)
9 Canadian town on Great Slave Lake (11)
14 Absolute government by one person (9)
15 Industrial city in NW Germany (9)
17 One from the asylum perhaps, a madman (7)
18 Walking-stick made from rattan palm (7)
20 Alternative spelling for an ear of maize (5)
21 Loch between Kinlochewe and Poolewe in NW Scotland (5)

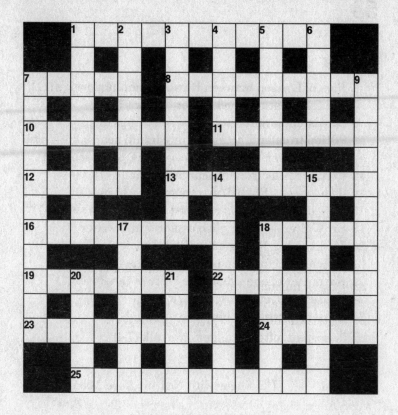

54

ACROSS

1 Part of London between Haringey and Redbridge (11)

7 Pentecost, seven weeks after Easter (7)

8 Scotland's largest city (7)

10 Ultimate extent, boundary or edge (5)

11 City on River Volga in W Russia, NE of Moscow (9)

12 Produced electrically charged particles (7)

14 James —— , English astronomer 1693-1762 (7)

15 —— link, something required to complete a series (7)

18 Sir Walter —— , English explorer and writer (7)

20 Member of a Protestant political society in Ireland (9)

21 Official call for purpose of inspection (5)

22 Supporter of one side in the Wars of the Roses (7)

23 French dialect of Belgium (7)

24 Variety of white or blue cheese (11)

DOWN

1 Slim —— , US singer with No1 hit *Rose Marie* in 1955 (7)

2 Franz —— , Hungarian composer (5)

3 Of flattery, say, sweet-sounding (7)

4 Countries of NW Africa collectively (7)

5 Province of NE South Africa (9)

6 Small bird of the genus Motacilla (7)

7 Real name of Buffalo Bill (7,4)

9 For many years he presented *Country Club* on Radio Two (5,6)

13 Upholder of the religious doctrines of a Swiss reformer (9)

16 Small finch-like bird (7)

17 Of an egg-cell or sperm-cell (7)

18 Road that goes round a town (7)

19 Operating on water near the coast (7)

21 Italian country house (5)

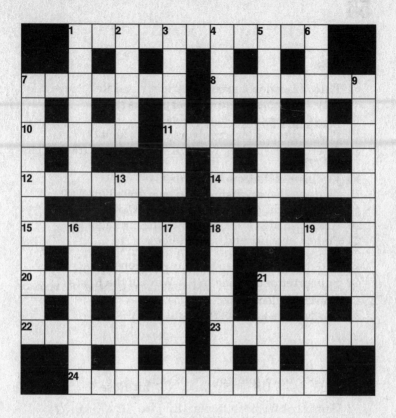

55

ACROSS

1 Tract of soft, wet ground (6)
4 & 10 Portuguese patron of explorers (5,3,9)
11 —— de chambre, a lady's-maid (5)
12 Place where rifles, revolvers etc are kept (7)
13 Alternative spelling for 20th letter of the Greek alphabet (7)
14 Violin or cello from Cremona (5)
15 Glass-walled enclosure used as a greenhouse (8)
18 Hollands gin chiefly made near Rotterdam (7)
20 Heavy wooden stick used by police in India (5)
23 French chemist and bacteriologist (7)
25 Moroccan port on the Strait of Gibraltar (7)
26 & 27 Flower seller in Shaw's *Pygmalion* (5,9)
28 The "syrinx", a wind instrument consisting of reeds or whistles of graduated lengths (3-5)
29 Person from Aden perhaps (6)

DOWN

1 County town and county of same name in NE Ireland (8)
2 Capital of Western Roman Empire 402-476AD (7)
3 Word derived from Italian for masters or young gentlemen (9)
5 Parliamentary proposal for consideration when business finishes in good time (5,3,6)
6 William ——, son of William the Conqueror (5)
7 Member of a religious and military order founded in 1119 (7)
8 Stage direction meaning they leave the stage (6)
9 Village, now in Humberside, site of a battle in 1066 (8,6)
16 Dish of cold meat or poultry served in jelly (9)
17 1st Earl of Beaconsfield 1804-81 (8)
19 This "sea" is a salt lake between SE Europe and Asia (7)
21 National emblem of Scotland (7)
22 Cost of maintenance (6)

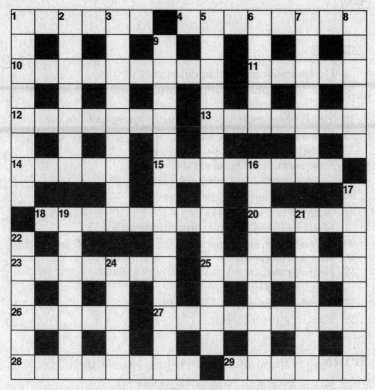

24 The third space in the bass or the first line in the treble, sung to a particular note in the first and fourth hexachords respectively, and a further note in the second and fifth (1-2-2)

56

ACROSS

1 Upset or overturned accidentally (8)
9 Nocturnal animal living on plains of Southern Africa (8)
10 Small case, especially one for keeping needles (4)
11 Rowdy spree or frolic (6-6)
13 Pretend or exaggerate illness (8)
15 Raw recruit in the army (6)
16 Disadvantage or drawback (4)
17 Member of cathedral chapter (5)
18 Winged leaf-stalk (4)
20 Medium-sized omnivorous monkey (6)
21 Grinding or pumping machine with a set of adjustable vanes or sails (8)
23 Scum or dregs (12)
26 Small shoot or branch (4)
27 Another name for a Viking (8)
28 Exulting proudly (8)

DOWN

2 Name for a motorway in Germany (8)
3 Winner of 16 Grand Prix races between 1951 and 1961 (8,4)
4 Series of short sharp turns (6)
5 Lower house of parliament of the Republic of Ireland (4)
6 Barred metal frame (8)
7 Ruth's husband in the Old Testament (4)
8 Carrying outwards from part of an organ (8)
12 Science of the animal body (12)
14 Begin again, recommence (5)
16 Serve a writ commanding attendance in court under a penalty (8)
17 Clear soup (8)
19 Sword bent like a sickle (8)
22 Papal messenger (6)
24 Tract of land devoted to agriculture (4)
25 Crossbar of a ladder (4)

57

ACROSS

1 English cabinetmaker and furniture designer (8)
6 Divide into two (6)
9 The Fate that holds the distaff (6)
10 Insect that transmits malaria (8)
11 Roman god of war who was later identified with the deified Romulus (8)
12 For a short time or period (6)
13 English painter noted for his informal portraits (12)
16 Singer who had a hit with *A Windmill in Old Amsterdam* in 1965 (6,6)
19 Farewell or goodbye (2,4)
21 East African country formerly Abyssinia (8)
23 Quarter of the circumference of a circle (8)
24 Choice piece of food, especially a small cake (6)
25 Size of paper cut to 10 inches by 8 inches formerly (6)
26 Any of a group of Semitic languages spoken in and near Syria (8)

DOWN

2 Very light colourless gas (6)
3 Revolving aerofoil (5)
4 Dame Sybil ——, British actress (9)
5 The goddess of retribution (7)
6 Port in SE Iraq (5)
7 Breed of sheep with short wool and greyish-brown face (9)
8 Detailed structure of a tissue as revealed microscopically (8)
13 Explosive mixture of saltpetre, sulphur and charcoal (9)
14 Solid eight-sided figures (9)
15 State capital of Hawaii (8)
17 Sluggishness, inactivity (7)
18 Ancient Egyptian wire rattles (6)
20 Fertiliser obtained from sea-bird manure (5)
22 British author of *Under Two Flags* (5)

58

ACROSS

1 Emil ——, Czech athlete, gold medallist (7)
5 Village at the foot of the Matterhorn not accessible by car (7)
9 More unusual, less common (5)
10 Adapted for seizing prey (9)
11 Mounted trooper (10)
12 Season leading up to Easter (4)
14 Tentative or speculative (12)
18 Atmospheric layer beginning about four and a half to ten miles up (12)
21 River flowing through York (4)
22 Seaman in the navy (10)
25 Racing sledge for two or more people (9)
26 Language spoken in the Netherlands (5)
27 Greek canal built between 1881 and 1893 (7)
28 American stock-farmer (7)

DOWN

1 Canton in NE Switzerland which bears the same name as its capital (6)
2 Grow strong and healthy (6)
3 Something that it baffling or confusing (10)
4 Tralee is the county town of this Irish county (5)
5 Book preceding Haggai in the Old Testament (9)
6 Crucifix or cross, especially one at the entrance to the chancel (4)
7 Liquorice-flavoured liqueur (8)
8 Outward sign that something is concealed (8)
13 Place of turbulent behaviour or disorder (4-6)
15 Railway engineering town just north of Southampton (9)
16 Type of acid more usually known as vitamin C (8)
17 Horizontal part of a goal (8)
19 Quick rough drawing in preparation for a more in-depth painting (6)
20 One who makes designs by eating out the lines with an acid (6)
23 Clear, upper air (5)
24 Flat open tart (4)

59

ACROSS

1 English preacher who founded Methodism (4,6)
6 Unsightly body fat (4)
9 Merriment, good-humour (10)
10 Another name for the kingfish (4)
12 Nightingale often mentioned in Persian poetry (6)
13 Large shop or trading centre (8)
15 Slang term for an expense account (7-5)
18 Medical person who specialises in heart (12)
21 Custom or idiom associated with Eire (8)
22 City on the West Bank of the Jordan (6)
24 & 25 Average number of years one is supposed to live to (4,10)
25 *See 24*
26 The gown worn by a Queen's counsel (4)
27 Opposite of ungentlemanly (10)

DOWN

1 Medicated lozenge to soothe a sort throat (6)
2 Interrupt a public speaker (6)
3 One of the two brothers who flew the first powered aircraft (6,6)
4 Channel Island where cars are banned (4)
5 Scientific study of insects (10)
7 Unevenly or poorly balanced (8)
8 Huge beast thought to be the hippopotamus in the book of Job (OT) (8)
11 In a regular or unchanging way (12)
14 Member of any of the W Germanic tribes that settled in Britain from 5th century AD (5-5)
16 In Greek mythology, his body was invulnerable, except for his heel (8)
17 Productive or prolific in bearing offspring (8)
19 Sultanate in NW Borneo which gained independence in 1984 (6)
20 Protein acting as a catalyst (6)
23 Longest river in Russia (4)

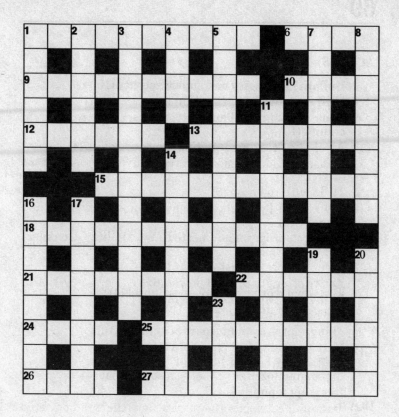

60

ACROSS

1 Hullabaloo, a noisy and showy activity (10)
6 Lord ——— , deputy prime minister 1989-90 (4)
9 Book containing Paul's letters used for reading in church (10)
10 Alcoholic drink made with honey and spices (4)
13 Measure of electromotive force equivalent to 1000 tons of TNT (7)
15 To do with the nose (6)
16 Old king of Pylos noted for his eloquence, wisdom and long life (6)
17 Holiday programme hosted by Judith Chalmers (4,3,4,4)
18 French impressionist painter (6)
20 Active strength or vital power (6)
21 Wiltshire town east of Melksham (7)
22 Dip biscuit in drink (4)
25 Thing that is a counterpart of another (10)
26 Narrow-bladed fencing sword (4)
27 English writer 1874-1936 (10)

DOWN

1 South American ostrich (4)
2 Relating to animal life (4)
3 Small place in Fife between Buckhaven and Leven (6)
4 A ——— —— —— ——, Dickens novel (4,2,3,6)
5 Tetragonal mineral found mainly in igneous rocks (6)
7 Too much, often abbreviated to OTT (4-3-3)
8 A fruit often used in winemaking (10)
11 Wiltshire town south-west of Melksham (10)
12 Disagreement of sound (10)
13 North American grasshopper (7)
14 Greek goddess of retribution and vengeance (7)
19 Characteristic flavour (6)
20 Italian city built on numerous small islands (6)
23 St ——— , village north of Land's End (4)
24 ——— Boht, actress in *Bread* (4)

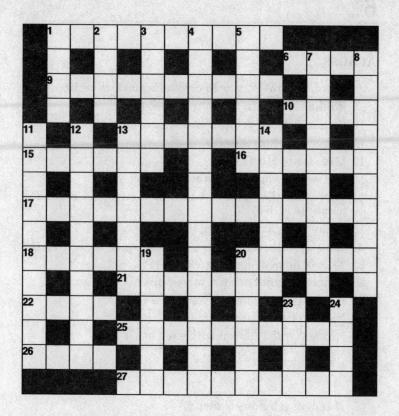

61

ACROSS

1 Second brightest star in constellation Orion (10)

6 Wading bird akin to the spoonbill (4)

10 Senior member of a profession or society (5)

11 Female sex-hormone (9)

12 Cage for poultry (3-4)

13 Old word meaning to form by carving (7)

14 Spores on the spikes of this fern resemble a snake's mouth-part (6-6)

18 In law, a right belonging to a property (12)

21 Like Cyclops, only having a single organ of sight (3-4)

23 Title of ancient Egyptian kings (7)

24 Officer who has care of sacred vessels in church (9)

25 Hindu kingdom in the Himalayas (5)

26 Native or citizen of Latvia (4)

27 Brought into relation with each other (10)

DOWN

1 N Indian religious leader (6)

2 Distressing, causing strain (6)

3 Irish folk-tune for *Danny Boy* (11,3)

4 Part of the universe in which life is possible (9)

5 Japanese dish consisting of small cakes of cold rice (5)

7 Admit unwillingly or with a bad grace (8)

8 Summaries or outlines usually of books (8)

9 Area of water between S Wales and SW England (7,7)

15 It gives one's pencil a point (9)

16 Musical by Rodgers and Hammerstein (8)

17 Short swinging upward blow (8)

19 One of a Hindu military caste claiming descent from Kshatriya, the warrior caste (6)

20 —— away, passed time without irksomeness (6)

22 The same again sometimes shortened to "do" (5)

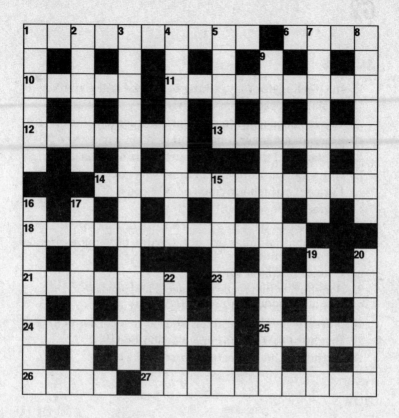

62

ACROSS

1 In Greek mythology, a king of Thrace and a monkey (6)
5 Roman emperor from 14-37AD (8)
9 Use long speeches to delay or obstruct legislation (10)
10 Story about superhuman beings of an earlier age (4)
11 Roman coin that was the fourth part of an as (8)
12 One without professional knowledge of a subject (6)
13 Former Spanish province on NW coast of Africa (4)
15 Segmentless worm (8)
18 Specified district in a French town or city (8)
19 Mathematical quantity not capable of being expressed in rational numbers (4)
21 County in Ulster (6)
23 Songbird which feeds on insects and seeds (8)
25 Acronym for petrol exporting countries (4)
26 Nursery-rhyme character who sat in a corner (4,6)
27 Brightest star in the constellation Bootes (8)
28 Author of the *Inspector Morse* books (6)

DOWN

2 Epigrammatic Japanese verse form in 17 syllables (5)
3 Device forcing water out of clothes without wringing (4-5)
4 Bubble-and—— , dish of potatoes and cabbage (6)
5 Play by William Shakespeare (5,10)
6 Sticky substance for catching feathered creatures (4-4)
7 Card-game based on collecting sets and sequences (5)
8 In South Africa, a foreigner or alien (9)
14 White or colourless mineral used in manufacture of glass, jewellery and enamel (9)
16 Woman leaving a will (9)
17 Goatsucker, a nocturnal bird (8)
20 Did some engraving (6)
22 Berkshire racecourse (5)
24 Heraklion is the capital of this Greek island (5)

63

ACROSS

1 Novel by R D Blackmore (5,5)

6 Border at one end (4)

9 Streak under the skin due to a blood leakage (5)

10 Board game played by one person (9)

12 US astronomer, born in Lahore, who won the Nobel Prize for Physics in 1983 (13)

14 American working on a stock farm (8)

15 Former female pupil or student (6)

17 —— Goldberg, actress in *Ghost* (6)

19 Mark at the back of a tennis court (4-4)

21 Non-technical name for the scapula (8-5)

24 `—— Morse', popular television series (9)

25 Edict having the force of law in Tsarist Russia (5)

26 River joining Severn south of Worcester (4)

27 Great symbolic battlefield of the Apocalypse (10)

DOWN

1 Matter discharged from a volcano (4)

2 Point of no return stream in N Italy (7)

3 French name for Aachen (3-2-8)

4 Glassy volcanic rock (8)

5 Stream or drain (5)

7 Fishing resort near Paignton (7)

8 Decider in a competition (3-7)

11 Waltz composed by Johann Strauss II (3,4,6)

13 Member of any fascist party or group (10)

16 Capital of Australia (8)

18 Thick-furred marsupial with a long snout (7)

20 Reykjavik is its capital city (7)

22 Compound of alcohol and acid (5)

23 William —— , English Quaker who founded a US state (4)

64

ACROSS

4 One who does menial or monotonous work for others (8)

8 Rhododendron-like shrub with showy flowers (6)

9 Art and skill of a sorcerer or magician (8)

10 Dome-shaped canopy used as protection against rain (8)

11 Self-possession or coolness (6)

12 Basis of measurement (8)

13 Lacking feelings such as sympathy and understanding (8)

16 Largest of the Shetland Islands (8)

19 Resort on the Isle of Wight (8)

21 —— Ness, sand and shingle area in Suffolk (6)

23 One buying goods from abroad (8)

24 Country formerly Siam (8)

25 Manufacture again (6)

26 Place where metal is separated from ore (8)

DOWN

1 Angular distance in astronomy or navigation (7)

2 Condensed roman printing type with a heavy face (9)

3 Spanish rice dish cooked and served in a large shallow pan (6)

4 Number 1 hit for Manfred Mann in 1964 (2,3,5,5)

5 Cold Spanish vegetable soup (8)

6 Precious stone occurring in hexagonal crystals (5)

7 Botanical name for heartwood (7)

14 Play or film with extravagant action and emotion (9)

15 Poisonous plant of the potato family once thought to have magical powers (8)

17 Isaac's father in the Old Testament (7)

18 Like some bacon, alternately fat and lean (7)

20 Bear that appears in comic strips (6)

22 Recess with a polygonal window (5)

65

ACROSS

8 Story with a symbolic meaning (8)
9 Dermapterous insect of the family Forficulidae (6)
10 Show a preference for something (3)
11 System of microphones and loudspeakers (8)
12 One who lends money at an exorbitant interest rate (6)
13 Humorous novel by Jerome K Jerome (5,3,2,1,4)
15 Seaport in Corsica, birthplace of Napoleon (7)
18 In football, illegally ahead of the ball (7)
21 Musical work by Haydn which includes *L'Ours*, *La Poule* and *La Reine* (5,10)
24 South American blanket-like cloak (6)
25 Language spoken in NW India (8)
26 Alcoholic drink containing beaten egg (3)
27 Large piece of landed property (6)
28 It is used as a point of reference in astronomy and navigation (8)

DOWN

1 Rectangular block at the base of a column (6)
2 Unperturbed, tranquil (6)
3 Officer in armed forces who is appointed from the ranks as a subordinate officer (3-12)
4 Cheyenne is the capital of theis NW US state (7)
5 1983 film, `Episode 6' of the *Star Wars* serial (6,2,3,4)
6 Old portable long-barrelled gun (8)
7 Plantation of grape plants (8)
14 Wedge-shaped indentation of the sea forming a drowned valley (3)
16 The green-eyed monster (8)
17 Idle talk or gossip (8)
19 —— Amin, former Ugandan leader (3)
20 Import or export illegally (7)
22 German physical chemist who formulated the third law of thermodynamics (6)
23 Lure into danger or embarrassment (6)

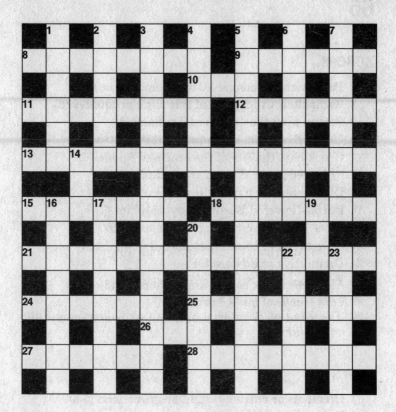

66

ACROSS

6 Patriotic song composed by Thomas Arne (4,9)

8 Kampala is the capital of this African country (6)

9 Person from the capital of Germany (8)

10 One of five digits on one's foot (3)

11 Greek city, the site of the oracle of Apollo (6)

12 Coloured paper thrown at weddings (8)

14 Older name for a metallic element, symbol Pt (7)

16 Purple-flowered European oyster-plant (7)

20 Piece of pork containing little meat (5,3)

23 Cure taken to counteract ill-feeling (6)

24 Diminutive of Edward (3)

25 Brazilian port, capital of Bahia state (8)

26 Sing in a quavering way (6)

27 *The King of Barataria*, operetta by Gilbert and Sullivan (3,10)

DOWN

1 Offshoots or cuttings might be grown in it (5-3)

2 Eucharistic offering (8)

3 Fenland town in Cambridgeshire (7)

4 Straight line over a vowel to indicate that it is long (6)

5 Salad plant similar to chicory (6)

6 Vicious animal that has separated from the main herd to live a solitary life (5-8)

7 Tune for hymn *O come all ye faithful* (6,7)

13 River flowing into Carrick Roads in Cornwall (3)

15 Surface for skating (3)

17 Hyena-like animal that mainly feeds on termites and carrion (8)

18 West Country county noted for its cider (8)

19 Thrust forward, stick out (7)

21 Critical report of a book, film or play (6)

22 Former Welsh county now part of Powys (6)

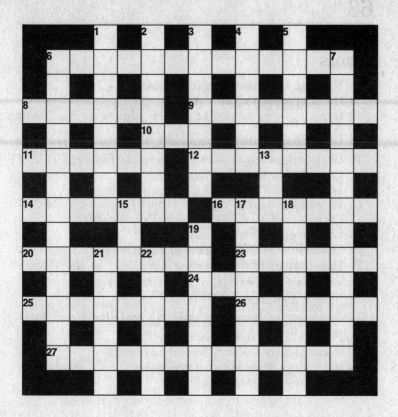

67

ACROSS

1 Married European lady in India (8)
5 German name for Gdansk (6)
8 Denis ——, presenter of *It'll be Alright on the Night* (6)
9 US rock singer born Robert Allen Zimmerman (3,5)
10 Drag someone by rope through water from one side of the vessel to the other (8)
11 Long, slender sword (6)
12 Phnom Penh is the capital of this SE Asian country (8)
13 Large social wasp of the family Vespidae (6)
15 Church caretaker and attendant (6)
18 One who deserts his career or country (8)
20 Devotion of prayers lasting nine days in the Roman Catholic church (6)
21 Bewitching fairy who rules over men's dreams in British folklore (5,3)
23 Nickname of Edmund II of England (8)
24 Foolish action or behaviour (6)
25 Vertical distance from bottom to top (6)
26 Very large diamond that has been part of the British crown jewels since 1849 (8)

DOWN

1 On River Svisloch, the capital of Byelorussia (5)
2 Pouch attached toa bicycle (9)
3 Official record of British Parliament (7)
4 Dish of cabbage and potatoes (6,3,6)
5 Prophetess and judge of Israel who fought the Canaanites (OT) (7)
6 Very large unspecified number (7)
7 Device for converting into electrical energy (9)
12 Henry ——, English physicist who discovered hydrogen (9)
14 Critical revision of a literary work (9)
16 Square pieces of pasta containing meat (7)
17 Practical person, one who faces facts (7)
19 One of the two official languages of Belgium (7)
22 Customer in a shop perhaps (5)

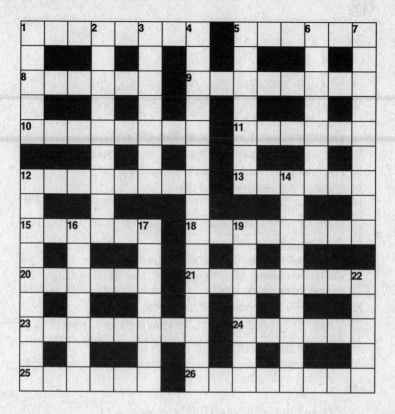

68

ACROSS

1 Removal of money from a bank account (10)

6 Elizabeth Talbot, Countess of Shrewsbury, known as —— of Hardwick (4)

9 Pessimist, one who believes the worst (5)

10 Carved article made by a sailor as a leisure activity (9)

12 Highest peak in Austria (3,797 metres) (13)

14 Flowed out or proceeded (8)

15 Ear of maize (6)

17 Rude or offensive remark or action (6)

19 A prompting or aide-memoire (8)

21 University student studying for a first degree (13)

24 Chart showing the heights of the land surface by means of contours (6-3)

25 Addictive drug obtained from poppies (5)

26 Type of photograph taken to check on an injury (1-3)

27 Shining like a heavenly body visible at night (4-6)

DOWN

1 Seaport in Caithness, Highland Region (4)

2 Terracotta figurine which takes its name from the town where it was made (7)

3 1957 film starring Dirk Bogarde (6,2,5)

4 Estimated or judged (8)

5 —— in Paris, 1952 film starring Doris Day (5)

7 Colourless volatile flammable alcohol (7)

8 Undertaker in Oliver Twist (10)

11 Hit for Stevie Wonder in 1969 (2,6,5)

13 Opera-oratorio in two acts by Stravinsky (7,3)

16 Rock-forming mineral (8)

18 Seats for clergy on the south side of the chancel (7)

20 Market ——, town near Peterborough (7)

22 Terms of reference given to an official or committee (5)

23 Speck of soot or dust (4)

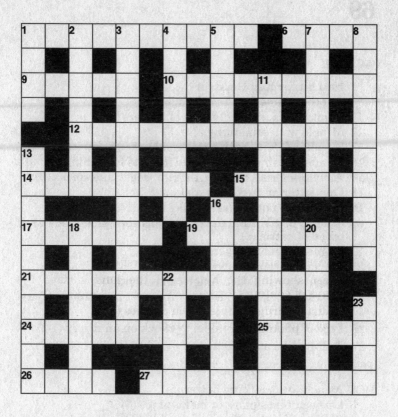

69

ACROSS

1 1964 hit for Ken Dodd (9)
8 Another name for the echidna (5,8)
11 Plant with scented clusters of flowers (5)
12 Mingle with something else (5)
13 Woodland deity with a tail and long ears (5)
16 Climbing palm or cane made from its long thin stem (6)
17 Alcoholic drink made with milk, sugar and spices (6)
18 Last letter of the Greek alphabet (5)
19 In music, a note to be held for its full time value (6)
20 County in NE England which has the same name as a breed of cattle (6)
21 Rogue or deceitful person (5)
24 Mediaeval type of oboe (5)
26 Large aquatic South American rodent (5)
27 Instrument which detects and records radioactivity (6,7)
28 Craft with twin parallel hulls (9)

DOWN

2 Attach to something larger (5)
3 Large public square or maketplace (6)
4 Public official authorised to administer oaths (6)
5 —— Flow, landlocked anchorage in the Orkney Islands (5)
6 Ionised region of atmosphere about 150 miles up (8,5)
7 West Indian batsman who often opened with Gordon Greenidge (7,6)
9 In music, to be played in an animated manner (9)
10 Of marrying only outside one's own group (9)
13 Gesture (often cocked) to express derision or defiance (5)
14 Greek letter (5)
15 Author who wrote The Cloister and the Hearth (5)
22 26 across or its fur (6)
23 Italian city where two gentlemen came from (Shakespeare) (6)
25 Volcanic or molten rock (5)
26 Hebridean island near Rhum (5)

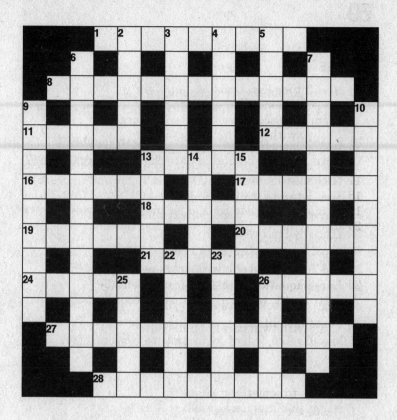

70

ACROSS

1 One of Robin Hood's companions (6,4)
6 NE Greek mountain where Otus and Epialtes tried to reach heaven (4)
10 Libreville is the capital of this African republic (5)
12 Until 1983, the capital of Cote d'Ivoire (Ivory Coast) (7)
13 Lack of red blood cells (7)
14 Sincere and enthusiastic (5-7)
18 Shooting skill of a specially trained soldier (12)
21 Wheedled or coaxed (7)
22 Saint's day celebrated in February 14th (9)
23 Old Testament book with only one chapter (7)
24 Literary word for inhabitant (9)
25 Style of Greek architecture (5)
26 Clarified buffalo butter (4)
27 Mixed salad dish of cooked meats, eggs, etc. (10)

DOWN

1 Deadlock or impasse (3-3)
2 City in north-west Iran formerly known as Tauris (6)
3 One of the main characters in *Treasure Island* (4,4,6)
4 Works or writings produced in childhood or youth of artist or author (9)
5 Game played on a board of 256 squares (5)
7 Fellow sailor (8)
8 Capital of South Australia (8)
9 Legally disqualifying (14)
15 Statistical graph using rectangles (9)
16 Honeycomb stitching (8)
17 Decide before hearing the whole case (8)
19 Kind of smoked haddock (6)
20 Fussy or pretentious (3-3)
22 Plain of alluvial deposits at mouth of river (5)

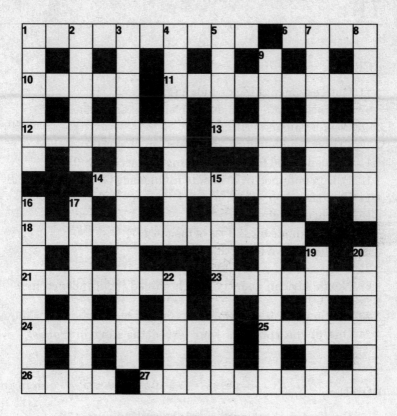

71

ACROSS

1 Old Testament king of Judah (11)
7 Five sisters of ——, mountains in western Scotland (7)
8 Peak or summit (7)
10 British equivalent of a N American diaper (5)
11 African lizard famous for changing its colour (9)
12 Poison obtained from deadly nightshade (7)
14 Huntsman's cry (5-2)
15 Fetched a higher price (7)
18 Absent-mindedness, loss of memory (7)
20 Lifelike, down-to-earth (9)
21 Deep wooded valley (5)
22 North African country which gained independence in 1955 (7)
23 Public speaker's platform (7)
24 One of the courtiers who served the king in *Hamlet* (11)

DOWN

1 Coniferous shrub with purple berry-like cones (7)
2 Of comparatively great weight (5)
3 Brittle element used in transistors, solar cells, etc. (7)
4 From one side to the other (7)
5 Lake District mountain (9)
6 Unsteady, rocky (7)
7 Rodent related to the jerboa (8-3)
9 Source of great and unexpected troubles (8,3)
13 Skin disease producing red scaly patches (9)
16 One who schools racehorses and prepares them for racing (7)
17 Alight from railway carriage (7)
18 One bringing a charge against another (7)
19 Entertainment business (7)

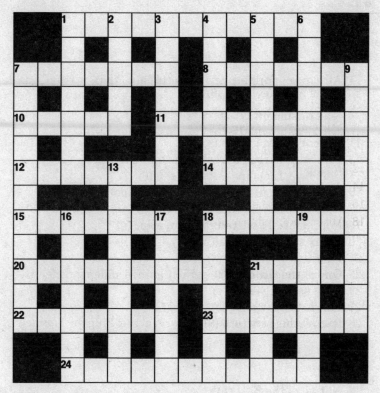

21 Flexible length of metal links (5)

72

ACROSS

1 Athenian philosopher who taught that virtue was based on knowledge (8)

9 All existing matter, energy and space (8)

10 State or royal treasury (4)

11 Author of *Lucky Jim* (8,4)

13 Fish with barbed dorsal spine on its tail (5-3)

15 Port near Lima in western Peru (6)

16 Sacred river in *Kubla Khan* (Coleridge) (4)

17 *Iliad* and *Odyssey* are attributed to this Greek poet (5)

18 Confidential assistant to a superior (4)

20 Flourish after a signature (6)

21 Familiar or pet title (8)

23 One of the *Goons* (5,7)

26 Arab sailing vessel (4)

27 Fabric made from goats' hair (8)

28 Recovering strength (8)

DOWN

2 Native of the East (8)

3 Seesawing toy (7-5)

4 British landscape painter (6)

5 Loitering with intent (4)

6 Device on vehicle for reducing sound (8)

7 Small alcoholic drink (4)

8 Town near Evesham in the county of Hereford and Worcester (8)

12 Festival celebrated on November 1st (3,6,3)

14 Republic in SW Arabia (5)

16 Atmosphere above the earth (8)

17 One who uses questionable and aggressive methods of selling (8)

19 Large bottle with a short narrow neck (8)

22 Fine worsted yarn (6)

24 — *of the D'Urbervilles* (Hardy) (4)

25 Give a sneering and suggestive look (4)

73

ACROSS

1 Old World songbird (8)

6 Hebrew prophet and judge in the Old Testament (6)

9 Latin for in the same place (6)

10 Start of a game of hockey (5-3)

11 One who can speak many languages (8)

12 Glenn ——, US bandleader (6)

13 Invisible observer (3,2,3,4)

16 One who imitates the character and mannerisms of another (12)

19 Monastery or convent (6)

21 Sportsman who fights in a ring (8)

23 Map line connecting places of equal temperature (8)

24 Red fruit eaten as a vegetable (6)

25 The last and worst part (3-3)

26 System of signs or symbols (8)

DOWN

2 His choice is take it or leave it (6)

3 Enid Blyton character (5)

4 Nepalese mountains (9)

5 Person from Lhasa (7)

6 City in Massachusetts, scene of execution of 19 witches in 1692 (5)

7 Pilgrim Fathers' ship (9)

8 Deprive of strength (8)

13 Seaport near Perth in Western Australia (9)

14 South-west African nomad (9)

15 Food of the gods (8)

17 Press reporter (7)

18 Falkland Island penguin (6)

20 Financial return (5)

22 Entice or lure (5)

74

ACROSS

1 14th century patriot who shot an apple from his son's head (7,4)

7 Organisms that damage crops (5)

8 Stupor induced by drug addiction (9)

10 Inclined towards or displaying love (7)

11 Former Canadian prime minister (7)

12 Eat small quantities, test the flavour (5)

13 Act on another's behalf (9)

16 Bend one's knee in respect (9)

18 West African gazelle (5)

19 Vital central point, core (7)

22 Having a more restless desire (7)

23 Groups of three sharing supreme power (9)

24 George ——, English novelist (5)

25 House where the Queen traditionally spends Christmas (11)

DOWN

1 US state on Lake Superior and Lake Michigan (9)

2 Agile or lithe (7)

3 Yeats's *Lake Isle* (9)

4 Excellence or worth (5)

5 An original curve in mathematics (7)

6 Longest river in France (5)

7 Line of English kings ruling from 1154 to 1485 (11)

9 Resting place of Noah's Ark (5,6)

14 Member of the hereditary aristocracy of ancient Rome (9)

15 10 across temperament (9)

17 Holder of a particular franchise or privilege (7)

18 Shakespearean play referred to as the "Scottish Play" (7)

20 Slang name for a carpenter (5)

21 Person engaged in a winter sport on the mountains (5)

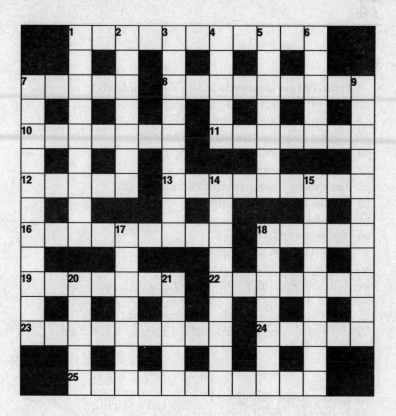

75

ACROSS

1 Over 700 coral islands in the West Indies (7)
5 Animal also known as the desert lynx (7)
9 Arranged in systematic form (7)
10 Back-handed sword-stroke (7)
11 Dapper or spruce (5)
12 Procession or parade (9)
13 Language closely related to Spanish (7)
14 Bright orange-red fabric (7)
16 Route plan (4-3)
19 Going away party (4-3)
22 Indian prince, ruler of a state (9)
24 Communion table at east end of a church (5)
25 Explanatory figure or plan (7)
26 Made a sound like dry leaves (7)
27 The dead variety of these plants do not sting (7)
28 Seed of an umbelliferous plant used as a condiment (7)

DOWN

1 Of the study of plants (7)
2 Natural home of a plant or animal (7)
3 Language of south-west India (9)
4 Arab or Syrian nomad (7)
5 Vehicle equipped to be lived in (7)
6 One of Sheridan's opponents? (5)
7 Privateering ship (7)
8 Slackest, least tight (7)
15 Person who solicits votes (9)
16 Ninth month of the Moslem year (7)
17 Transversely or sidewise (7)
18 Loose-fitting nightclothes (7)
19 Shaped like a circular solid figure, perfectly round (7)
20 Current moving away, discharge (7)
21 Physicist whose discoveries led to the invention of the dynamo (7)
23 Of the country, rustic (5)

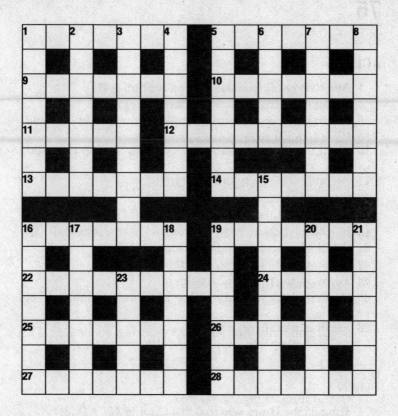

76

ACROSS

1 Ape that is like a human being in form (10)
6 Flat-bottomed boat used for freight (4)
9 Instrument for measuring angles when surveying land (10)
10 Sixth month of ecclesiastical year in Jewish calendar (4)
12 Second largest city in Pakistan (6)
13 Situated at inner or attached end (8)
15 Cloth or soft paper for blowing into (12)
18 Idle hanger-on at social events and gatherings (6-6)
21 Small Mediterranean flowering shrub (4-4)
22 Upper part of the windpipe, the voice-box (6)
24 Town on west coast of Alaska (4)
25 Garden plant with tall spikes of (usually) blue flowers (10)
26 Small mountain lake (4)
27 Achievement, accomplishment (10)

DOWN

1 King of the Huns who invaded Gaul in 451 AD (6)
2 Develop or cut a milk tooth (6)
3 Author of *King Solomon's Mines* (5,7)
4 Wealth regarded with contempt (4)
5 Short instrumental piece (10)
7 Bogota is the capital of this South American country (8)
8 Animals and birds etc that are not tame (8)
11 An embitterment or a making something worse (12)
14 Person between childhood and adulthood (10)
16 Single-reeded woodwind instrument (8)
17 Flat box-like stringed instrument (8)
19 It gives the author's name under the title or heading (6)
20 Free from liability (6)
23 Hebrew measure for dry goods (4)

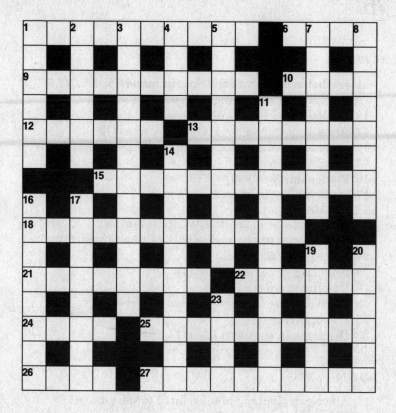

77

ACROSS

1 English composer of the *Sea Symphony*, in 1910 (7,8)
9 Considering something in a specified way (9)
10 Debbie —— , Paul Daniels' assistant (5)
11 Allow someone to have what they want (7)
12 Edible shellfish with a pair of fan-shaped shells (7)
13 Small Old World bird (3)
14 Plunge into water (7)
17 —— *Nights*, another name for the *Thousand and One Nights* (7)
19 Brightest star in the constellation Carina (7)
22 Hotel porter or page (chiefly North American) (7)
24 *Ben* —— , 1959 film (3)
25 Hold closely in one's arms (7)
26 Umpire or referee (7)
28 English name for a South American river (5)
29 Postmeridian (9)
30 Headland in southern Iberia (4,2,9)

DOWN

1 American climbing-plant related to the vine (8,7)
2 Exhorted, entreated (5)
3 Athlete in an obstacle race (7)
4 Natural simplicity, artlessness (7)
5 Nourishment taken into the body (7)
6 Preliminary propositions in mathematics (7)
7 Shark with very large fins (5-4)
8 One who invests money in a business without taking part in the running of it (8,7)
15 Highest peak in the Alps (4,5)
16 Old French coin of low value (3)
18 Female sandpiper or ruff (3)
20 Inactive medical substance (7)
21 The whole matter or affair (7)
22 Lucky dip container (4-3)
23 Monrovia is the capital of this African country (7)
27 Freshwater fish of the salmon family (5)

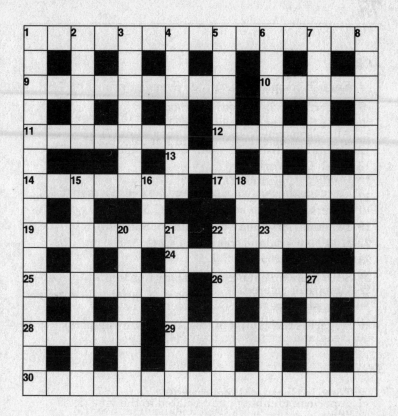

ACROSS

1 Pursue an advantage closely (6,2)

6 Eastern warehouse or storeroom (6)

9 To be performed slowly (music) (6)

10 & 11 Final defeat of Napoleon I in 1815 (6,2,8)

11 *See 10*

12 Plymouth —— , football team (6)

13 Towards the bottom right-hand corner of a map (5-7)

16 Came together to help someone (7,5)

19 Sweet dessert wine from southern Spain (6)

21 & 23 New Zealand soprano (4,4,2,6)

23 *See 21*

24 Scandinavian country with many fjords (6)

25 Another name for the pawpaw, a large yellow or orange fruit (6)

26 Hobart is the capital of this Australian island (8)

DOWN

2 Town in Greater Manchester (6)

3 John —— Baird, Scottish television pioneer (5)

4 Isopod crustacean with a flattened segmented body (9)

5 Classical bagpipe music (7)

6 Coagulated milky latex of some tropical trees (5)

7 Greatly pleased, extremely satisfied (9)

8 Bird that perches on trees but usually sings on the wing (8)

13 Volcanic vent emitting gases only (9)

14 Structures on each side of arch ends (9)

15 Cuban dance in 2-4 time (8)

17 Emitting rays, beaming with joy (7)

18 Great wild sheep of Asia (6)

20 City in southern Turkey, capital of province of the same name (5)

22 Buddhists' and Hindus' principle of retributive justice (5)

79

ACROSS

1 Bathroom powder (6)
4 French red wine (8)
8 Large silvery game fish (6)
9 Unit of power (8)
10 Lumpy pudding or sweetmeat (8)
11 Reduce in quality (6)
12 Diplomatic etiquette (8)
13 US state in the central Pacific Ocean (6)
15 Son of Daedalus who flew too near the sun (6)
18 Practice of fighting with fists (8)
20 High quality grape brandy (6)
21 Jamb (8)
23 Iced drink containing rum, lime juice and sugar (8)
24 One of the Knights of the Round Table (6)
25 Old Chinese table game (3-5)
26 Second largest continent (6)

DOWN

1 Companion of Paul (New Testament) (5)
2 Electrical device used for storing electric charge (9)
3 Small Asian deer with a bark-like cry (7)
4 Flan named after a town in Derbyshire (8,7)
5 Explorer who introduced potatoes to England (7)
6 Famous American waterfalls (7)
7 Soft malleable silvery element (9)
12 Sovereignty of a monarch's son (9)
14 Ability to control one's actions (9)
16 Great pain or distress (7)
17 Part cut off from the main body (7)
19 SE US state, capital Atlanta (7)
22 Kingdom of more than 150 islands in the SW Pacific (5)

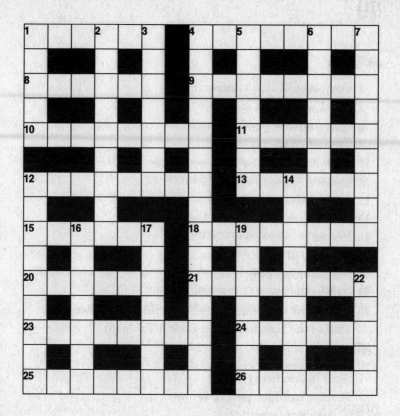

80

ACROSS

1 Composer of *The Planets* (5)

4 Short, squat gun (8)

8 Non-commissioned officer below a sergeant (8)

9 Seaport in east China (8)

11 Steel-making town by River Dee in N Wales (7)

13 Seaport and bay in SW Spain (9)

15 Large evergreen trees mentioned in the Bible (6,2,7)

18 Of a mythological king of Corinth (9)

21 100 lepta in Greek currency (7)

22 Mutual agreement (8)

24 Man-made object, for example a tool or work of art (8)

25 South American tree-dwelling animal (8)

26 Voucher worth a stated amount of money (5)

DOWN

1 Skill in conjuring (5-5)

2 Former word for port or left (8)

3 French pavement (8)

4 Dutch painter who painted *The Laughing Cavalier* (4)

5 Tending to create peace (6)

6 Harp-like musical instrument (6)

7 Aniseed-flavoured spirit of E Mediterranean (4)

10 Region of northern Scotland (8)

12 French emperor who was defeated at Waterloo (8)

14 Small bird of the swallow family (4-6)

16 Capital of Hungary (8)

17 Old Testament boat (5,3)

19 River flowing into the Bristol Channel (6)

20 Canal linking the Atlantic and Pacific Oceans (6)

22 Hollow round vessel for holding liquor (4)

23 Placed under a social prohibition (4)

81

ACROSS

1 North American marmot (9)

6 Chief Anglo-Saxon god (5)

9 Resort and city in NW Mexico (7)

10 Ball-game played on a board (9)

11 Lessening of tension between nations (7)

12 Became less rigid (7)

13 Descriptive name often given to Kent (6,2,7)

18 Shrub with drooping flowers (7)

20 British colony in NW Atlantic (7)

22 Striped timber of a Guianan tree (5-4)

23 Reappearance of ancestral characteristics (7)

24 Bound by a pledge (obs.) (5)

25 Government official who investigates complaints (9)

DOWN

1 Organisation that closely monitors operations (8)

2 One who protests against something (8)

3 Coloured pencil (6)

4 Lacking power (6)

5 Indian rice dish (8)

6 Form of phlebitis which can occur after childbirth (5-3)

7 Having some part doubled (6)

8 The smaller of neptune's two satellites (6)

14 Subjected to a domineering influence (8)

15 Story (often Biblical) set to music (8)

16 Tank containing fish (8)

17 Interpreter or guide in eastern countries (8)

18 Damp firework (6)

19 Round loaf of bread (6)

20 Smear over (6)

21 Hero of the Charlemagne legend (6)

82

ACROSS

1 Sydney is the capital of this Australian state (3,5,5)
7 Disciple who denied Jesus three times (5)
8 Profession of Jesus's earthly father (9)
9 Genus of water-lilies (7)
10 Defect, flaw or stain (7)
11 Language of ancient Rome (5)
12 Nom de plume (9)
14 Equine animal used to transport goods and equipment (9)
17 IOW resort and regatta town (5)
19 Public room at a health resort (7)
21 Italian physicist and astronomer 1564-1642 (7)
22 *The Lake Isle of* —— (Yeats) (9)
23 Arnos ——, station on Piccadilly Line (5)
24 He played the son in *Steptoe and Son* (5,1,7)

DOWN

1 Folded sheet of writing paper (7)
2 Labourer (7)
3 Beat more strongly than usual (5)
4 Saturday and Sunday (7)
5 Scottish region that includes Edinburgh (7)
6 Author of *Utopia* (3,6,4)
7 Actress in *To the Manor Born* (8,5)
8 Butcher's cleaver (7)
13 Ornamental centrepiece (7)
15 One who investigates into the cause of death (7)
16 Gossip or rumour (7)
17 Eau de ——, perfumed liquid (7)
18 Leave as a gesture of disapproval (4,3)
20 Poem that can be set to music (5)

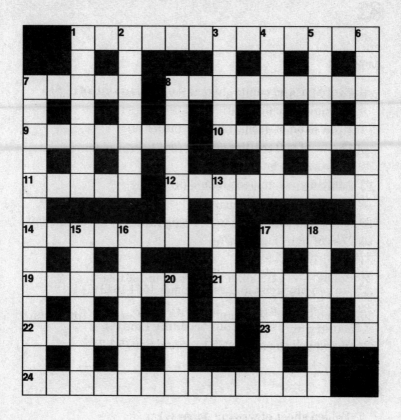

83

ACROSS

6 Paul McCartney hit about a Scottish headland (4,2,7)

8 Autonomous board (6)

9 Town in central Mali (8)

10 *The —— and the Pendulum*, 1961 horror movie (3)

11 Layers of rock (6)

12 Publican, a seller of alcohol (8)

14 One hundredth of a mark (7)

16 Salad plant used as a coffee substitute (7)

20 Loss of hair, baldness (8)

23 Sensitive layer of the eye (6)

24 Bobby —— , US singer with hits in 1961-3 (3)

25 Bird-life of a region (8)

26 Belmopan is the capital of this Central American country (6)

27 One of the *Goons* (5,8)

DOWN

1 Green-skinned banana-like fruit (8)

2 In Ecuador, it's the world's highest active volcano (8)

3 Wooden or plastic pin (7)

4 Of aphorisms or pithy sayings (6)

5 Old place of execution in London (6)

6 Biblical hill between Bethany and Gethsemane (5,2,6)

7 Presenter of *That's Life!* (6,7)

13 Samuel's teacher (Old Testament) (3)

15 Scottish word for no (3)

17 Blue campanulaceous flower (8)

18 Study of cells in attempt to detect abnormal ones (8)

19 Former duchy and kingdom in Germany (7)

21 Seabird with parrot-like beak (6)

22 Rocky ravine in North America (6)

84

ACROSS

6 Physical basis of life (**10**)

8 & 7 Reformed prostitute befriended by Jesus (**4,9**)

9 *Guy* —— , one of Walter Scott's Waverley novels (**9**)

11 Division of a tribe (**4**)

12 Greyish-brown horse (**3**)

13 Daughter of Priam with unheeded gift of prophecy (**9**)

16 Member of woodwind section (**4**)

17 Nearly lost a pound of flesh to Shylock! (**7**)

18 See **22**

20 Two gallons (**4**)

21 Musical US state (**9**)

23 Doctor for the BBC! (**3**)

24 Swedish pop group and palindrome meaning "father" (**4**)

25 Those cut from the hedge (**9**)

29 Soft French cheese (**4**)

30 Australian tree providing oil (**10**)

DOWN

1 Short Henry Wood concert (**4**)

2 Old English school (**4**)

3 Often semi-circular church recess (**4**)

4 Queen of England (**7**)

5 Remnant of fictional planet deadly to Superman! (**10**)

7 See *8 across*

8 Wrongly-applied names (**9**)

10 Keystone of the Welfare State (**3**)

13 Archbishopric founded by Augustine (**10**)

14 One effect of atomic explosion (**5,4**)

15 Greek philosopher (**9**)

19 Turkish town, early home of Christianity (**7**)

22 & 18 Of its own kind in Latin in textbooks (**3,7**)

26 African country (**4**)

27 Union for cleric workers and others (**4**)

28 Predatory gull (**4**)

85

ACROSS

1 Actor in *Carry On* films (7,8)
9 Design printed in relief (7)
10 Devon —, was a Derbyshire and England cricketer (7)
11 Town north of Montgomery in Mid-Wales (9)
12 Of a nobleman (5)
13 Ornament worn between head and torso (7)
15 Surfeit, complete fulness (7)
17 Another name for the marsh-marigold (7)
19 With gradually decreasing tone and speed (music) (7)
21 Ravine or water-course (5)
23 Chemical fertiliser (9)
25 Orchestral kettledrums (7)
26 Student who fails to complete an academic course (4-3)
27 Twin sons of Leda (6,3,6)

DOWN

1 British prime minister three times between 1923 and 1937 (7)
2 Of the kidneys (5)
3 Person addicted to excessive drinking (9)
4 City in SE Michigan on river of the same name (7)
5 Legendary founder of Rome and its first king (7)
6 Cold dish of raw vegetables (5)
7 Australian actor in *Rumpole of the Bailey* (3,6)
8 Famous Cup Final venue (football) (7)
14 Scottish quarter-day on 2nd February (9)
16 Camera lens that magnifies distant objects (9)
17 Relating to or caused by motion (7)
18 Mild powdered seasoning from red pepper (7)
19 Full of people (7)
20 Impose too great a strain (7)
22 Texan siege and massacre (5)
24 Coral reef (5)

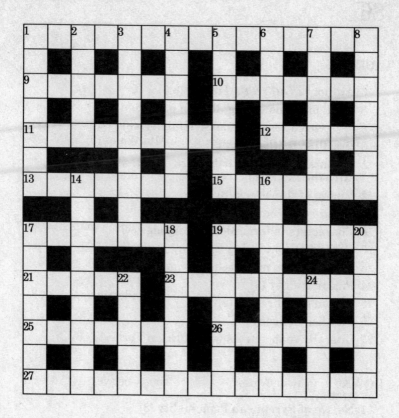

86

ACROSS

6 Author of *Gulliver's Travels* (8,5)

8 Light machine giving illusion of motion (6)

9 "—— to catch woodcocks" (Hamlet) (8)

10 Brazilian football city (3)

11 Mountains where Noah's Ark reputedly came to rest after the Flood (6)

12 Victim of shipwreck (8)

14 Nature of 2's bat for England (7)

16 Characters in formation of languages (7)

20 Cathedral containing Epstein's sculpture of Christ (8)

23 Person whose name is not given (6)

24 Picean conifer (3)

25 Italian film director (8)

26 Flat-fish delicacy (6)

27 Literally soap actress wife of Brian Forbes! (7,6)

DOWN

1 Native of Pyrennean Principality (8)

2 He was the cricket captain of England (8)

3 Cushion for kneeling (7)

4 Egyptian God of the Dead (6)

5 Composite plant of the aster family (6)

6 Means of achieving aircraft motion (3,10)

7 Novel by F Scott Fitzgerald (3,4,6)

13 Rocky height (3)

15 US address reference to state above Kentucky (3)

17 French city with wonderful cathedral (8)

18 Line of equal temperature during coldest time (8)

19 Holder of commission in Army (7)

21 Creed named after early Christian Council declaration (6)

22 Related on the father's side (6)

87

ACROSS

1 Exact observance of etiquette (9)

8 Jurassic fossil bird (13)

11 Town in Fife west of St Andrews (5)

12 King's companion in Anglo-Saxon England (5)

13 Alternative spelling for a Malay sailing-vessel (5)

16 Projectile that can be observed in flight (6)

17 Slang word for piano (6)

18 Dagger signs in printed matter (5)

19 **20,000** ——s *Under the Sea* by Jules Verne (6)

20 Largest of the Channel Islands (6)

21 City and resort in SE Florida (5)

24 Alfred —— , poet 1880-1958 (5)

26 Small protuberance or excrescence (5)

27 Operetta by Johann Strauss junior (3,10)

28 Port on Chesapeake Bay in Maryland (9)

DOWN

2 Official who shows people to their seats (5)

3 Roman general, statesman and historian 100-44BC (6)

4 Full of mischief (6)

5 Chemically inactive (5)

6 Art of deciphering codes etc. (13)

7 Large carnivorous dinosaur (13)

9 Colourless gas used in welding (9)

10 Unit of frequency equal to 1,000,000 hertz (9)

13 Introduction, preface or prelude (5)

14 Betel-nut (5)

15 Where Stanley met Livingstone in 1871 (5)

22 Use a syringe, inoculate (6)

23 Collection of curiosities (6)

25 Capital of Bulgaria (5)

26 Official language of Cambodia (5)

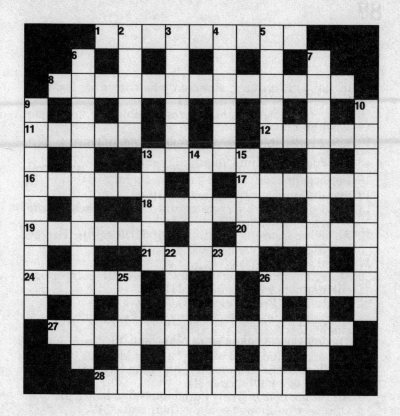

88

ACROSS

1 In the 19th century, a person who traded with plains Indians of SW North America (10)
6 The government ministry responsible for food, etc (1,1,1,1)
10 The plastic by which gramophone records are collectively known (5)
11 The whole body of the nothern Buddhist canonical writings (9)
12 Small denomination German coins (8)
13 An order of Greek architecture characterized by the volute of its capital (5)
15 An old measure of length, about 71-76 cm, in Turkey and Russia (7)
17 Aural pain (7)
19 Molecules consisting of one or several polypeptide chains containing amino acids (7)
21 White-faced French clown (7)
22 The tennis player who won the 1989 French men's singles (5)
24 The Windward island whose capital is Bridgetown (8)
27 The expression "God willing" among Muslims (9)
28 Any bird of the *Gruidae*, large wading birds (5)
29 The call of a public crier (4)
30 An Italian dish of finely cured uncooked ham (10)

DOWN

1 The runner who won the 1984 men's Olympic 10,000m gold (4)
2 A public, written declaration of a political party's intentions (9)
3 Polymeric amide formed into a fibre (5)
4 One of the Khatti or Heth, an ancient people of Syria (7)
5 Book or record published again (7)
7 —— Delon, star of the 1970 movie *Borsalino* (5)
8 In chess, the placement of a bishop on N2, with a pawn on N3 (10)
9 A kind of ornamental metallic lacework (8)
14 White coffee made frothy with pressurized steam (10)
16 Character or symbol in writing that stands for a concept (8)

18 A black, web-footed, gluttonous seabird that breeds on cliffs (9)

20 Pertaining to mistiness (7)

21 One of the *Three Musketeers* (7)

23 Side division of the nave of a church (5)

25 In computing, a binary code representing characters (1,1,1,1,1)

26 The Mexican currency (4)

89

ACROSS

1 In Spain and Portugal from the 13th century, a noble of the most highly privileged class (7)
5 One of the major five flat horse-races for three-year olds (7)
9 Eye specialist (15)
10 Modified underground stem without scale leaves, from which a crocus grows, for example (4)
11 Take in to graze for payment; a burden or tax (5)
12 The Israeli seaport town, north of Haifa (4)
15 A subphylum of arthropods having a distinct head, thorax and abdomen (7)
16 N American Indian of an Algonquin tribe, now mostly in Oklahoma (7)
17 A fever transmitted by a protozoan parasite, carried by mosquitos (7)
19 Any of several highly esteemed food-fish of the family *Sparidae* (7)
21 The Roman emperor from 54 AD to 68 AD (4)
22 Shares or stock, collectively (5)
23 The thread across which the weft is woven (4)
26 Inflammation of the stomach and intestines (15)
27 A collection of pus in a cavity (7)
28 The hit 1972 musical movie starring Liza Minnelli (7)

DOWN

1 An Italian dish consisting of small dumplings (7)
2 The fatty degeneration of the middle coat of the arterial wall (15)
3 British children's author and short-story writer (4)
4 Speeches given in praise (7)
5 King of Lydia, famed for his wealth (7)
6 A mainly S African genus, consisting mostly of trees and shrubs of the lily family (4)
7 Adhesive covering for wounds (8-7)
8 In valves and tubes, the source of electrons (7)
13 The fruit of the oak (5)
14 A glossy black varnish or lacquer (5)
17 The capital of Nicaragua (7)
18 The —— , a long-running radio soap opera (7)
19 A nerve issuing from the lower part of the spinal cord (7)

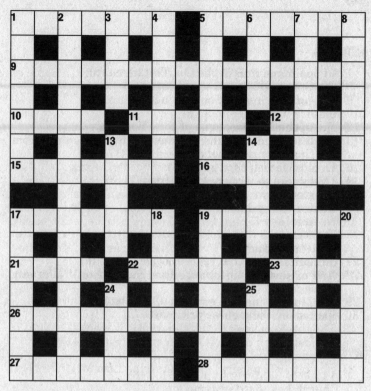

20 Lay something away (7)

24 A North American Indian tribe (4)

25 A nebula in the constellation Taurus (4)

90

ACROSS

1 A book of maxims in the Old Testament (8)
5 The Greek lyric poetess of Lesbos (6)
9 Non-positive remark or action (8)
10 Spanish national dance (6)
12 One of the five boroughs of New York City (9)
13 The last stage of an insect's development (5)
14 The first king of Israel (4)
16 An old Spanish card game (7)
19 A very thin pastry enclosing fruit (7)
21 The stem of various small palms (4)
24 Musical composition whose principal subject recurs in the same key (5)
25 The members of a secret republican society in Italy in the 19th century (9)
27 Unicellular, asexual reproductive bodies (6)
28 Well-mannered libertine, after Richardson's *Clarissa* (8)
29 Band consisting of a single multi-instrumentalist (3-3)
30 Spanish or Portuguese princesses (8)

DOWN

1 A type of lightweight plaited hat (6)
2 Church keyboard instruments (6)
3 A run in cricket not coming from the bat (5)
4 The Rochester suburb which gave its name to reformatories (7)
6 The ending of black slavery in the US (9)
7 A group of six stars visible to the naked eye, in the shoulder of the constellation Taurus (8)
8 Medium-sweet Spanish sherries (8)
11 A children's card game (4)
15 A northern constellation lying between Cassiopeia and Pegasus (9)
17 Coffee made in a machine giving high extraction under pressure (8)
18 The 7-time National Hunt champion jockey (8)
20 The wingless parasitic insects, *Pediculi* (4)
21 Preparatory drawing to be reproduced as a painting etc (7)
22 A dark-coloured igneous rock and type of pottery (6)
23 Northern sea-ducks, sought after for their down (6)
26 The last letter of the Greek alphabet (5)

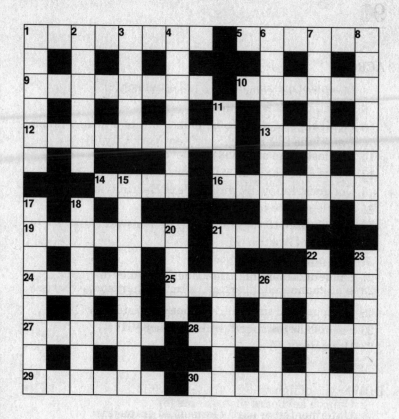

91

ACROSS

1 Meaningless, complicated language (5-5)
6 Colloquial name for the BBC (4)
9 Small slips of wood to be picked out of a heap without disturbing others (10)
10 Musical composition (4)
13 White sauce or soup made from stock (7)
15 Conquest following the Battle of Hastings (6)
16 Edible marine bivalve mollusc (6)
17 It is phrased to suggest the desired answer (7,8)
18 Capital of Austria (6)
20 Port adjoining Liverpool (6)
21 Small ornament of little value (7)
22 Point on plant stem from which leaves grow (4)
25 Compound of tin, lead, antimony and sulphur (10)
26 —— of Cleves, fourth wife of Henry VIII (4)
27 Dramatist (10)

DOWN

1 Unfermented or partly fermented grape-juice (4)
2 Letters, packets etc (4)
3 Owners of or workers on a rig (6)
4 Its action or effect is unpredictable (7,8)
5 —— Mussolini, Italian Fascist leader (6)
7 Resident in a foreign country (10)
8 Escaped convict in Australia (10)
11 Play by Chekhov (5,5)
12 End of the world battle in Revelation (10)
13 Actively courageous (7)
14 Mark on wings of certain butterflies (3-4)
19 Scottish county in Stathclyde Region (6)
20 Slang word for a drunken spree (6)
23 Crosby the crooner & film actor (4)
24 'The Garden of England' (4)

ACROSS

1 Chief town on the Isle of Anglesey (8)

5 German composer of the *Messiah* (6)

9 French author of *Gargantua* and *Pantagruel* (8)

10 Downhill ski-race with obstacles (6)

11 Wooing (8)

12 Narcotic or sedative drug (6)

14 Icicle-like pendant in a cave (10)

18 Holiday lecture on film (10)

22 Slow, graceful dance in triple time (6)

23 English writer of evocative verse for children (2,2,4)

24 Yellow pigment found in egg-yolk (6)

25 Meteoric matter in fine particles (8)

26 Grass-cutting implement (6)

27 Duke of Milan in *The Tempest* (8)

DOWN

1 Quintus Horatius Flaccus, Roman poet (6)

2 Pangs of efforts of childbirth (6)

3 Rocksalt, chemical formula NaCl (6)

4 Estrangement, a turning away (10)

6 Pimento or Jamaica pepper (8)

7 Part of Croatia near the Adriatic Sea (8)

8 University town in Dyfed (8)

13 Double —— , type of cheese (10)

15 Something that acts as an incentive (8)

16 Chief support (8)

17 OT prophet (8)

19 Sign of the Zodiac (6)

20 River flowing from the Black Forest to the Black Sea (6)

21 Prefix meaning towards the right (6)

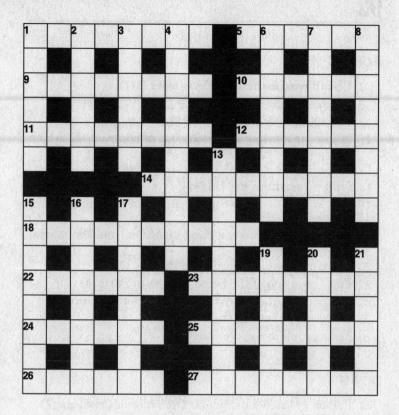

ACROSS

7 No-toll road for fast traffic in the US (7)

8 Czech composer *The Cunning Little Vixen* opera (7)

10 The **40**th president of the US (6,4)

11 In law, any wrong not rising out of contract for which there is a remedy by damages (4)

12 A small book stitched, but not bound (8)

14 Callow recruit in the US (6)

15 *The* —— ——; a work by Brendan Behan set in a prison (5,6)

19 In Greek mythology, a King of Athens and the mortal father of Theseus (6)

20 The treatment of disorders of the foot (8)

22 Pont ——; one of the Seine bridges in Paris (4)

23 A former English and Yorkshire cricket captain (5,5)

25 A Cheshire town on the Mersey (7)

26 Main group in a cycle race (7)

DOWN

1 Person granted a particular franchise or privilege (7)

2 The chief feminine deity of Olympus (4)

3 One of a fierce people from NE Germany who overran Gaul, Spain, N Africa and Rome (6)

4 Meaningless refrain in songs (3,2,3)

5 A class of asymmetrical molluscs with a broad, flat foot (10)

6 The name of both a US and ex-Soviet state (7)

9 The capital of Trinidad & Tobago (4,2,5)

13 A tense in grammar (10)

16 The Liberal prime minister **1894-5** (8)

17 Revoke at cards (7)

18 A Lancashire town with a soccer team (7)

21 Jewish prophet who survived the lions' den (6)

24 A SE Asian republic bordering Thailand, Cambodia and Vietnam (4)

94

ACROSS

7 The capital of Mongolia (4,5)

8 Small room with a polygonal window (5)

10 In South Africa, urban settlement for non-whites (8)

11 The birth place of writer Isaac Asimov (6)

12 —— buco; the Italian dish for shin of veal (4)

13 Asti ——; an Italian sparkling wine (8)

15 An infectious fever with red spots (7)

17 Members of the *Arachnida* class (7)

20 The first man to reach the South Pole (8)

22 The army bugle call for lights out (4)

25 The capital of Turkey (6)

26 The ——; a newspaper launched by Robert Maxwell (8)

27 Member of a flower calyx (5)

28 The country whose capital is Managua (9)

DOWN

1 A Fife town and soccer club in the Scottish 2nd division (5)

2 The pineapple (6)

3 Basil ——; film actor who played Sherlock Holmes (8)

4 Instrument for finding directions (7)

5 In heraldry, a symbolic armband (8)

6 An order of insects with half-leathery, half-membranous wings (9)

9 The official literary language of Pakistan (4)

14 A labiate herb with aromatic, bitter and stomachic properties (9)

16 Realgar, the resin of a Moroccan conifer (8)

18 An England batsman and cricket administrator (5,3)

19 Lack of haemoglobin (7)

21 The green cormorant (4)

23 A genus of trees of the willow family (6)

24 The ——, the Dutch seat of government (5)

95

ACROSS

1 An American edentate with bands of bony plates (9)
8 A European principality, sovereign since 1866 (13)
11 The smallest letter in the Greek alphabet (4)
12 The ancient Egyptian ram-headed god (5)
13 Pierce ——; The writer who founded a sports journal in 1824, the forerunner of the *Sporting Life* (4)
16 A form of vacuum or Dewar flask (7)
17 Curtis ——; The US Open golf champion 1988 and `89 (7)
18 A bivalve shellfish with a distinctive shape (7)
20 4 to 6 week old chicken served whole (7)
21 The US comedian, born Eltham London 1903 (4)
22 A jeer (5)
23 The ex-Soviet Union telegraph agency (4)
26 They lie in the sea between Italy and Greece, owned by the latter (6,7)
27 The Italian composer of over 600 harpsicord sonatas (9)

DOWN

2 The former lyricist for Andrew Lloyd Webber (4)
3 The Greek goddess of the hunt (7)
4 Type of rock produced by solidification of magma (7)
5 An old stringed instrument shaped like a half-pear (4)
6 A small resort on the West Sussex coast (13)
7 A group of US and UK territories in the Caribbean near Puerto Rico (6,7)
9 The influential German philosopher who wrote *The Will to Power* (9)
10 The Scottish town at the end of the Moray Firth (9)
14 Gladstone ——; England fast bowler in the early 1990s (5)
15 Wernher von ——; The German rocket pioneer (5)
19 A light beer (7)
20 A former state of N. Central Europe (7)
24 A bluish-white metallic element (4)
25 Philosopher born 20. down 1724, who wrote the *Critique of Pure Reason* (4)

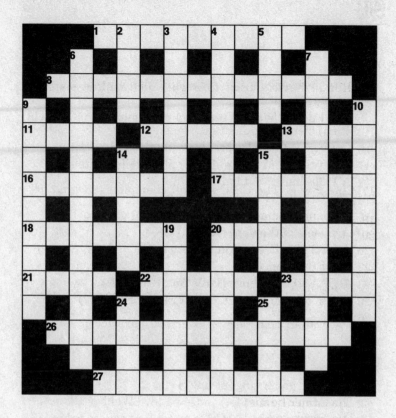

96

ACROSS

7 Rift in Earth's crust through which molten material erupts (7)

8 The English World Formula 1 champion who also held 4 IoM TT titles (7)

10 Conventionalised representation (10)

11 A physical and mental Hindu philosophy system (4)

12 A 1960s puffed-out hairstyle (8)

14 The Greek goddess of wisdom (6)

15 Inflammation of the cleft of the upper gullet (11)

19 A muscle of the upper arm (6)

20 A form of coffee-making machine (8)

22 A son of Adam (4)

23 & 26 A soprano born Barcelona 1933 (10,7)

25 Warm coastal district, eg of France or Italy (7)

26 *See 23*

DOWN

1 The card game vingt-et-un (7)

2 The Maple genus (4)

3 An African republic which was a Portuguese colony (6)

4 A language of north-west India (8)

5 A poison got from nux vomica seeds (10)

6 —— Yevtushenko; A provocative Russian poet born 1933 (7)

9 The World Formula 1 champion 1988, '90 and '91 (6,5)

13 Gabriel D. ——; The inventor of a thermometer scale (10)

16 A Mediterranean labiate shrub used in cooking (8)

17 The African republic founded in 1822 by freed US slaves (7)

18 In law, intentional attempt to use violence to do bodily harm (7)

21 Blaise ——; The 17th century French philosopher and scientist (6)

24 The currency of various Arabian states, eg Oman (4)

97

ACROSS

7 The tactic of delaying, and avoiding battle (9)
8 Popular name for a number of marine gastropods (5)
10 23 12 & 25 A novel by Muriel Spark about a charismatic schoolmistress (3,5,2,4,4,6)
11 A region of SE Europe comprising NE Greece, S Bulgaria, and W Turkey (6)
12 See 10
13 US motor racing vehicles (4,4)
15 Winner of the 1992 Portuguese Formula 1 GP (7)
17 A green pear-shaped fruit (7)
20 Gradual blindness caused by excess internal eye pressure (8)
22 A play written by Joe Orton (4)
25 See 10
26 Judith ——; A television presenter (8)
27 Peter ——; 1960s NZ Olympic gold medallist runner (5)
28 The English illustrator known for his posters and *Yellow Book* pictures (9)

DOWN

1 Russian country house (5)
2 Nun's folded head-dress (6)
3 Collectively, the old Greeks and Romans (8)
4 Gallic cartoon character (7)
5 Pertaining to the chest (8)
6 Current conductor terminal (9)
9 Horse-breeding establishment (4)
14 Female theatrical dancer (9)
16 Ring-dances (8)
18 The French author and philosopher who wrote *Candide* (8)
19 In baseball, the player who fields behind the batter (7)
21 Joint chairman of the Yugoslav peace conference (4)
23 See 10
24 The author of *The Female Eunuch* (5)

98

ACROSS

7 The Open golf champion, 1992 (4,5)

8 & 18 19th century American author of macabre short stories (5,5,3)

10 The "Cornhusker State" of the USA (8)

11 Balm made from the mountain tobacco plant (6)

12 & 19 One of the "Moors Murderers" (4,7)

13 In Greek mythology, the flier whose son flew too close to the sun (8)

15 *See 1 down*

17 Name of a series of Egyptian pharaohs (7)

20 Italian violin virtuoso and composer who extended the instrument's compass (8)

22 Joe ——, famous English dance orchestra leader (4)

25 A restraint imposed on outdoor movement (6)

26 Author of *The Ginger Man* (8)

27 & 9 Historical theatre street of London (5,4)

28 Royal Naval dockyard (9)

DOWN

1 Formula 1 world champion, 1992 (5,7)

2 A reef of rock (6)

3 —— Plan, US programme to aid European economic recovery after World War II (8)

4 US film director, responsible for *The Pink Panther* series (7)

5 Singer of number one pop hit *Well I Ask You*, 1961 (4,4)

6 Canadian city and island (9)

9 *See 27 across*

14 Amorous conduct guide written by the Indian Vatsyayana sect (4,5)

16 American university (8)

18 *See 8 across*

19 *See 12 across*

21 USA state whose capital is Des Moines (4)

23 Treeless plain of SE Europe and Asia (6)

24 Gland in which eggs are produced (5)

99

ACROSS

1 Members of the Muslim empire of India 1526-1857 (3,6)
8 Artist who drew over-ingenious contraptions (5,8)
11 Parliament of Eire (4)
12 One of *The Three Musketeers* (5)
13 English county in the early 1990s now part of Somerset (4)
16 Fourth US president and New York avenue (7)
17 Feudal Japanese knight (7)
18 Traditionally the aristocratic West End of London (7)
20 A pirate, or privateering ship (7)
21 River of north-east England (4)
22 Membrane which hangs from the soft palate (5)
23 A musical composition (4)
26 English author born in France who wrote *The Bad Child's Book of Beasts* (7,6)
27 British island in the South Atlantic used as US air base (9)

DOWN

2 Shere ——, American researcher & author (4)
3 —— Moor, first decisive battle in the English Civil War (7)
4 Grinling ——, sculptor who carved the choir stalls in Wren's St Paul's (7)
5 A member of the cat family (4)
6 Poet Laureate 1967-72 (5,3-5)
7 —— SW, was Nicholas Budgen's constituency (13)
9 18th century Scottish founder of the classical school of economics (4,5)
10 & 24 US legislation to control monopolies (4-5,4)
14 On the Nile, one of the world's largest dams (5)
15 Hard mineral, variety of corundum, used for polishing (5)
19 In meditation, an undirected train of thoughts (7)
20 Largest island of East Indonesia (7)
24 *See 10*
25 A counter-tenor (4)

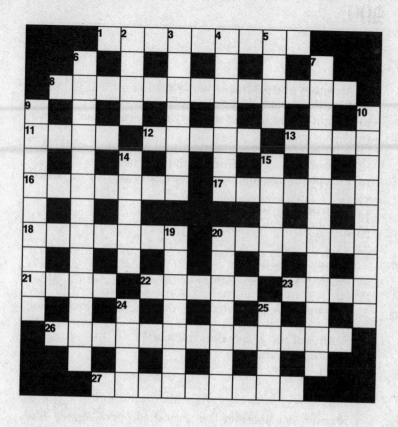

100

ACROSS

7 An actor who played James Bond (7)

8 A mathematical proposition (7)

10 Knighted English actor, playwright, composer and wit (4,6)

11 A hollow tumour containing fluid or soft material (4)

12 Author of the book *Gone with the Wind* (8)

14 European kingdom, not a member of the EC or NATO (6)

15 Oath of medical ethics (11)

19 European republic with a population of about 57 million (6)

20 Author of the book *Saturday Night and Sunday Morning* (8)

22 Spanish surrealist painter of *Dog Barking at the Moon* (4)

23 One-time prime minister of the Yugoslav Federation (5,5)

24 Author of the James Bond novels (7)

25 Capital of Guinea (7)

DOWN

1 Russian composer of the unfinshed opera *Prince Igor* (7)

2 Indigo plant or dye (4)

3 In 1993 he was the Conservative Secretary of State for National Heritage (6)

4 Previous name of Zimbabwe (8)

5 Italian composer & cellist 1743-1805, often compared to Haydn (10)

6 Lexicographer who compiled *The American Dictionary of the English Language* (7)

9 North Antrim town and bay (11)

13 Scottish mountain range (10)

16 Italian region whose capital is Turin (8)

17 System of relief typing for the blind (7)

18 17th century French comedy playwright and actor (7)

21 Author of *White Fang* (6)

24 —— sea; the world's fourth largest lake (4)

101

ACROSS

8 French novelist, author of Nana (4)
9 Brother and lyricist of George Gershwin (3)
10 Subsonic tactical missile used in the Falklands War (6)
11 Modified leaf forming the gynaeceum of a flower (6)
12 Russian-born US composer, pianist & teacher, composer of the Lysistrata Suite (8)
13 Commander of the American Expeditionary Force, 1917-18 (7,8)
15 Western action to overcome the Soviet blockade of Berlin (7)
17 Fertile mixture of decomposed organic substances (7)
20 French artist (1864-1901) famous for his Moulin Rouge scenes (8,7)
23 A werewolf (8)
25 Spanish novelist 1867-1928 (6)
26 19 & 28 Irish playwright and critic (1856-1950) (6,74)
27 A fabulous bird (3)
28 See 26

DOWN

1 Latin lyric poet (6)
2 British water speed record holder (8)
3 US novelist, winner of the 1949 Nobel Prize, who wrote The Reivers (7,8)
4 An old motor-car or aeroplane (7)
5 Italian painter and Renaissance genius (8,2,5)
6 Illicitly made liquor (6)
7 Abominable snowman (4)
14 A brownie or friendly goblin (3)
16 Nation of SE Nigeria (3)
18 20th century Italian composer of the opera Il Cordovano and general musical works (8)
19 See 26
21 Town and region of the Scottish southern uplands (6)
22 A bird which sings a night (6)
24 The gorse genus (4)

102

ACROSS

7 A drug used to relieve pain (9)
8 Surveyor of the Queen's Pictures who was divested of his knighthood (5)
10 Organ responsible for the production of insulin (8)
11 German leader of the Protestant reformation (6)
12 Name of a series of rulers of the Holy Roman Empire (4)
13 The Battle of ——; a naval engagement in the Greek War of Independence, 1827 (8)
15 A harmonious condition of society in which government is abolished as unnecessary (7)
17 A teacher of rhetoric in ancient Greece (7)
20 English writer born in Hungary, who wrote amongst others *The Ghost in the Machine* (8)
22 'Hawkeye State' of the USA (4)
25 American space exploration project of the 1960s (6)
26 15th century Italian painter whose masterpiece was the *St Lucy Altarpiece* (8)
27 Government set up by Marshal Petain (5)
28 18th century Italian painter of *The View on the Grand Canal* (9)

DOWN

1 US golfer who won more than 80 PGA tournaments (5)
2 A vote of assent in a governing body (6)
3 Gigantic animal described in the Book of Job (8)
4 Plant of the araliaceous genus *Panax*, cultivated for its restorative properties (7)
5 Ancient Greek essayist and biographer (8)
6 Scottish county town on the Moray Firth (9)
9 A member of Europe's largest ethnic and linguistic group (4)
14 Republic comprising more than 3,000 islands and 250 tongues (9)
16 Italian composer (1879-1936) of *The Fountains of Rome* (8)
18 Conflict between Great Britain and China, resulting in the ceding of Hong Kong to Britain (5,3)
19 Canadian prime minister who proposed the Constitution Act which gave Canada complete independence (7)
21 A retreat of a wild animal (4)

23 Inventor of the triangular rotor internal-combustion engine (6)

24 Explorer who died in 1912 in an effort win the race to the South Pole (5)

ACROSS

1 Mountain traveller's long spiked staff (10)
6 A character placed on the stave to fix the pitch of the notes (4)
9 Highwayman who made a legendary ride to York (4,6)
10 A body of Zulu warriors (4)
13 Illicit pecuniary share (4-3)
15 eg Apache, Cree (6)
16 A hunting expedition in Africa (6)
17 Humperdinck's opera based on a fairy tale (6,3,6)
18 The muse of comedy and pastoral poetry (6)
20 Goose's mate (6)
21 The 15th and 16th books of the New Testament (7)
22 Alfred Gilbert's statue in Piccadilly Circus, London (4)
25 Ifs and buts (10)
26 "All is but ——; renown and grace is dead"(*Macbeth*) (4)
27 Houdini practised it (10)

DOWN

1 Verdi opera set in Egypt (4)
2 —— and shovel (4)
3 —— Detroit, character in *Guys and Dolls* (6)
4 Brecht & Weill's work based on *The Beggar's Opera* (10,5)
5 Dover's are white, according to the Vera Lynn song (6)
7 Season which starts on August 1 with the feast of the first fruits (10)
8 Genus of the lily family which has given its name to several butterflies of a similar pattern (10)
11 Main thoroughfare of a town (4,6)
12 Toothache (10)
13 Toasted cheese on toast (7)
14 Turf between the tee and the putting green (7)
19 Very large passenger jet aircraft used for short flights (6)
20 Poor quarter—the word comes from the Jewish sector in Venice (6)
23 Marco ——, explorer (4)
24 To see at a distance (4)

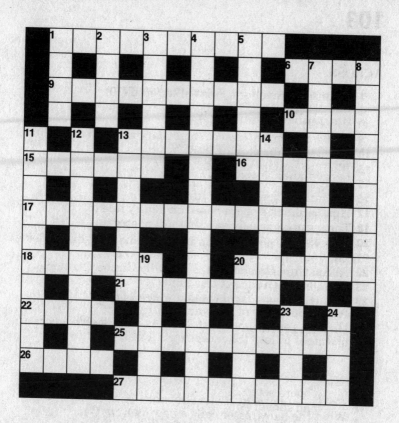

104

ACROSS

1 Unfurnished inn for travelling companies in Eastern
countries (12)
8 Diminutive diminutive (3)
9 Lower Jurassic (7)
11 Idiomatic Welsh phrase frequently used by Shakespeare's Fluellen in *Henry V* (4,3)
12 Large Indian antelope (7)
13 Archaic song or division of a poem (5)
14 Where you might find Freddie in a cinematic night-
mare (3,6)
16 eg Two draft-horses (9)
18 —— Rouge, power group in Cambodia now disbanded
(5)
20 eg Apaches, Cree etc (7)
22 The Derby is a race of this kind (7)
23 Samuel Butler's ideal commonwealth (7)
25 A cloth measure of 1.25 yards (3)
26 "In thy youth thou wast ——/As ever sigh'd upon a
midnight pillow"(Shakespeare's AYLI) (2,4,1,5)

DOWN

1 *Cold —— Farm* by Stella Gibbons (7)
2 What the hairdresser calls a new hair-cut (7)
3 Small puff pastry cases (3-2-4)
4 Synthetic fibre which gave its name to leg coverings
(5)
5 Military shoulder-piece (7)
6 Midas was given the ear's of this animal as a punishment (3)
7 What the 'trouble and strife' is, according to the old 15
song (4,2,2,4)
10 Bram Stoker's vampire (5,7)
15 Max Miller was a star of this (5,4)
17 Michael ——, Labour's Minister for the Environment
(7)
18 Ukranian city on the river Donets (7)
19 He practises a system of kneading treatment on painful muscles (7)
21 What Francis Drake did to the King of Spain's beard
in 1587 (5)
24 S (3)

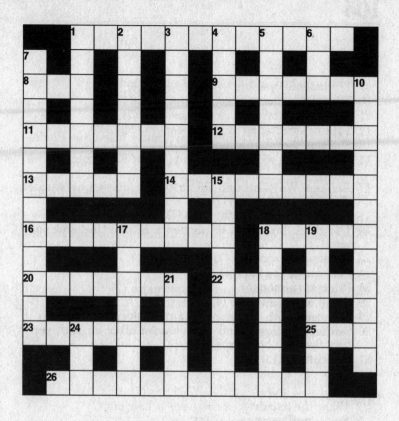

105

ACROSS

1 Traditional opening to a story (4,4,1,4)
10 Whitaker's has printed one since 1869 (7)
11 Sort of illusion such as *trompe l'oeil* (7)
12 Type of skirt worn by cheer-leaders (2-2)
13 She was thoroughly modern (5)
14 Cutting tool with arched blade set at 90 degrees to the handle (4)
17 Ancient West Iranian idiom of the Sassanide period (3rd-7th century AD) (7)
18 Pertaining to an earthquake (7)
19 The thick laying on of pigments in painting and pottery (7)
22 Cinderella's admirer (7)
24 Perform in the lists (4)
25 Pilgrim's pouch (5)
26 Small mountain lake (4)
29 Cetacean with a large projecting tusk (7)
30 Garden flowers which were named after an 18th century Swedish botanist (7)
31 Of printing (13)

DOWN

2 The governor of a nome (7)
3 Eternities (4)
4 Composer of *Turandot* (7)
5 Chinese pasta (7)
6 Jacques ——, French comic actor and film maker (4)
7 Smooth road surface made from small broken stones (7)
8 Making over-fine distinctions (13)
9 Insomnia (13)
15 A very light wood (5)
16 A piebald horse (5)
20 A lady's saddle-horse (7)
21 Pertaining to kissing (7)
22 Put together from parts already made (5,2)
23 Fluty-toned musical toy (7)
27 Go away! (4)
28 Once it would have been Siamese (4)

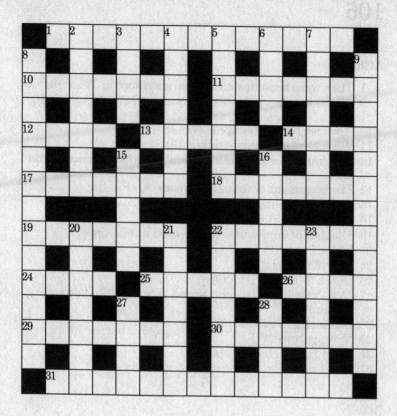

ACROSS

1 They were used in a cinematic massacre in Texas (9)
9 Ritual murder by Kali's followers in 19th century India (7)
10 A variety of winter apple (7)
11 What the law is proverbially (3)
12 & 4 Author of *Rosencrantz and Guildenstern are Dead* (3,8)
13 The treatment of foot ailments (9)
15 Puts into `solitary' (8)
16 Large South American vulture (6)
18 Number of copies of a book issued at one time (7)
21 Little finger (6)
24 Sheriff's officer (8)
26 Dutch South African (9)
27 "—— met by moonlight, proud Titania" (Shakespeare's *Dream*) (3)
28 Batsman's dismissal (3)
29 Mosque tower (7)
30 From Italy's chief sea-port (7)
31 Instrument for measuring precipitation (4-5)

DOWN

2 "——, —— it's off to work we go"(Dwarves' song, Disney's *Snow White*) (5-2)
3 Covered (7)
4 *See 12 across*
5 Dogs and cats which have no home (6)
6 aka Il Duce (9)
7 Agitated (mus.) (7)
8 The disreputable or unpleasant aspect (5,4)
14 Female (side) (7)
16 Case containing charge for a gun (9)
17 Female sex hormone (9)
19 Snakelike (8)
20 Like a particular semi-precious stone (7)
22 Famous US falls (7)
23 One sunk the *Titanic* (7)
25 The first person of the Trinity (6)

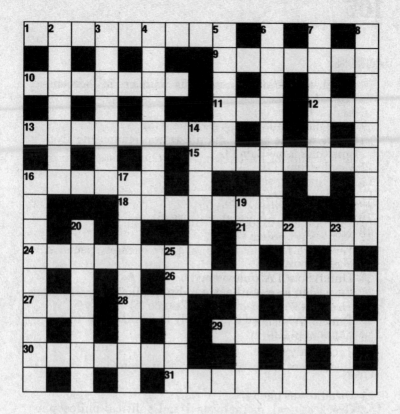

ACROSS

1 Dutch town now synonymous with an EC agreement (10)
6 Lady's fingers (4)
9 First name of Popeye's girlfriend (5)
10 Name for the bodily manifestation emanating from a spiritualist medium (9)
12 Kettledrums (7)
13 —— and Buy sale (5)
15 Milliners accessory (7)
17 Rod for measuring cloth (7)
19 Sort of bonds associated with Ernie (7)
21 Nazi secret police (7)
22 The more familiar name of a tax exempt special savings account (5)
24 Thin flat loaf of unleavened bread in Asia (7)
27 Vespasian's amphitheatre in Rome (9)
28 —— de ville, a town hall in France (5)
29 Type of sauce used extensively in Chinese cuisine (4)
30 Replicated (10)

DOWN

1 Othello was one (4)
2 Greek ethical, metaphysical and political philosopher (384-322BC) (9)
3 A bathing establishment in Classical times (5)
4 Country which had a general election this year on November 25th (7)
5 The Biblical Uriah was one (7)
7 Drab cloth used for military uniforms (5)
8 The final conflagration (10)
11 One of them has no toes according to Edward Lear (7)
14 They are used for eating Chinese food (10)
16 "I think I could turn and live with ——, they are so placid and self-contain'd," (Walt Whitman: Song of Myself) (7)
18 Describing a reversion to primitive type (9)
20 Heavy Cuban knife (7)
21 The science of language (7)
23 The pride of Gracie Field's alley (5)
25 Greenfly (5)
26 Enid Blyton's policeman Mr —— (4)

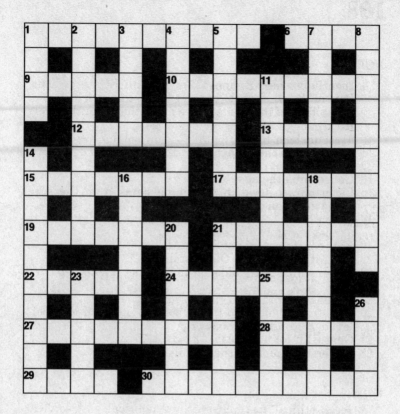

108

ACROSS

1 Lighthouse near Swansea (7)
5 Part of inn where beer is served from the cask (3-4)
9 Inhabitant of the vast steppes of northern South America (7)
10 Museum keeper (7)
11 —— Port on the Manchester Ship Canal (9)
12 Inuit home (5)
13 Concerning the nose (5)
15 Latin phrase used in reckoning dates from the supposed creation of the world (4,5)
17 A small 18th century armchair of curved design; a light carriage with two wheels (9)
19 East coast province of South Africa (5)
22 The 34th book of the Old Testament (5)
23 Novel which is an addenda to Paul Scott's *Raj Quartet* (7,2)
25 Ointment for the hair (latinised) (7)
26 Something embedded in the body tissue such as a pellet containing a hormone (7)
27 Gentle bit for a horse (7)
28 Understatement for rhetorical effect (7)

DOWN

1 English hills and water (7)
2 Childhood spotty disease (7)
3 Last year's football league champions (5)
4 Nickname given to Thomas Jonathan Jackson, legendary American Confederate general (9)
5 Fastening or clasp (biblical) (5)
6 Date-plum (9)
7 Bunting, common in Europe and considered a great delicacy (7)
8 Inventor of wireless telegraphy (7)
14 Recurring theme associated with a person or a thought (9)
16 —— author of *The Day of the Locust* (9)
17 The name of the second brightest star in the sky (7)
18 Western province of Czechoslovakia proverbially home of unconventional folk (7)
20 Eponymous TV detective series set in Glasgow (7)
21 Distances swum in swimming pools (7)
23 Famous WW1 battle (5)

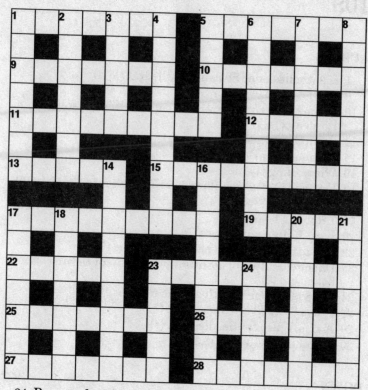

24 Process data into a computer (5)

109

ACROSS

1 & 9 Architect of St Paul's cathedral (11,4)
9 *See 1*
10 Name given to the French beaches running south from Bordeaux (4,7)
11 Scandinavian thunder-god (4)
14 Isambard –– Brunel (7)
16 White of egg (7)
17 French river which flows past Verdun into Belgium (5)
18 Dhoti or ——-cloth (4)
19 1 Robin's bear (4)
20 West Indian witchcraft (5)
22 Musical work which precedes a fugue (7)
23 Dance band instruments of gourds containing dried beans etc (7)
24 Gaseous element with atomic number 10 (4)
28 Prove by trial or experiment (11)
29 A small case for needles etc. (4)
30 Novel by H G Wells (3,8)

DOWN

2 Peter Pan's opponent (4)
3 The same (Latin) (4)
4 A cross-beam (7)
5 A boy attendant (4)
6 Make a baron, etc. (7)
7 England's cricket captain (6,5)
8 Give the vote (11)
12 It opens most locks (8,3)
13 Composition by Verdi (5,6)
15 Opera singer who gave her name to a peach dessert (5)
16 Eponymous tea-growing area (5)
20 Divan; empire (7)
21 Jump-jet (7)
25 Ukrainian capital (4)
26 Most insignificant chess man (4)
27 French policemen (slang) (4)

110

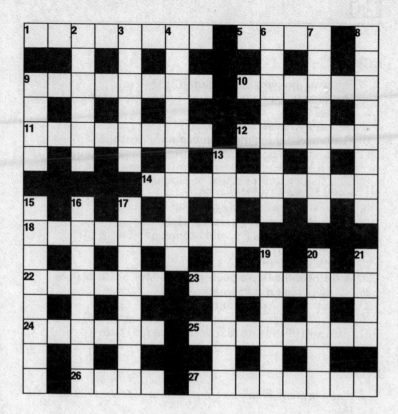

111

ACROSS

5 Spicy or savoury condiment (6)
8 Pre-metric standard size of paper measuring 22 x 30 inches (8)
9 Self-denying, strict hermit (7)
10 Author of *La Divina Commedia* (5)
11 In rowing, fencing etc a supplementary competition in which losers get a second chance to get to the final (9)
13 The theory and practice of eloquence as taught in Ancient Greece and Rome (8)
14 Bicycle for two people (6)
17 Seventh letter of the Greek alphabet (3)
19 It has the symbol Sn, and atomic number 50 (3)
20 Go-between (6)
23 Knick-knack (8)
26 & 5 Pre-Raphaelite poetess and sister of 10, 29 (9,8)
28 Slang name for a pawnbroker (5)
29 Angel of the Annunciation (7)
30 In a solid, regular three-dimensional shape (8)
31 Thane of ——, was Macbeth's original title (6)

DOWN

1 The eminent lyric poet of Ancient Greece (522-443BC) (6)
2 Instrument like a small harpsichord (7)
3 Occasions when there is no whip imposed in Parliament (4,5)
4 African expedition (6)
5 *See 26 across*
6 Old name for a doctor (5)
7 Familiar name of the disease *Herpes zoster* (8)
12 European monetary unit (3)
15 The largest region of Spain (9)
16 Name given to drink of alcoholic spirits served with ice and water or soda in a tall glass (8)
18 They are used to secure camping accommodation (4-4)
21 Fellow of a college (3)
22 The hub of a nuclear power station (7)
24 Half the diameter of a circle (6)
25 Units for reckoning the payment of gas (6)
27 Scanty garment worn by Muslim pilgrims nearing Mecca (5)

112

ACROSS

1 Decorative needlework (10)
9 The concluding passage of a musical piece, often forming an addition to the basic structure (4)
10 London area thought to be named by the fact that Edward III kept hunting hounds there (4,2,4)
11 Person he gains unauthorised access to computer's data (6)
12 Container as a flying toy (3,4)
15 Specimen of proficiency at 1 (7)
16 When the sails press against the mast of a sailing ship (5)
17 Sea eagle (4)
18 A measure for fresh herrings (4)
19 Natural chambers of cavities in the body, especially in bone (5)
21 Pleasantness of sound, harmony (7)
22 Dutch humanist and leading scholar of the Renaissance (7)
24 Author of *A la Recherche du Temps Perdu* (6)
27 Pertaining to government by a small group of people (10)
28 Artless, unsophisticated person (4)
29 A hand at bridge at which there is no card higher than a nine (10)

DOWN

2 Deer whose glands produce a strong-smelling reddish brown substance used as a perfume ingredient (4)
3 Small South African antelope which gave its name to a brand of trainer (6)
4 Historically the title given to the eldest daughter of the monarch of Spain or Portugal (7)
5 Title taken by the Bishop of York (4)
6 Muslim woman's veil (7)
7 A bumptious little person; a children's jumping game (10)
8 Circles of darker coloured-grass caused by the outward spread of fungus (5-5)
12 Apiculture (3-7)
13 Deep dislike of foreigners (10)
14 A kind of heavy dark wood furnished by various species of Diospyros (5)

15 A set of twenty (5)
19 The science of the bodily structure of animals and plants (7)
20 A member of a Native American people of the Plains, now living mainly in Oklahoma and Wyoming (7)
23 —— Panza, companion to *Don Quixote* (6)
25 A platform extending from the shore into the water (4)
26 Dynasty which ruled China from 1368 to 1644 (4)

113

ACROSS

1 English composer (1659-95) (5,7)
9 Gun holder (7)
10 Small stringed instrument (7)
11 Clarified buffalo butter used in Indian cuisine (4)
12 Madagascan arboreal primate (5)
13 Aromatic herb used in curing and pickling (4)
16 Harem attendants (7)
17 Pitt the ——, prime minister (1783-1801, 1804-6) (7)
18 Steak ——, dish of raw minced beef with seasonings (7)
21 They rule during the minority, absence or disability of sovereigns (7)
23 Common name of acquired immune deficiency syndrome (4)
24 Sir Henry ——, otherwise known as Hotspur (1364-1403) (5)
25 A Muslim prince, chieftain or governor in the Middle East (4)
28 The obscuring of one celestial body by another (7)
29 Betrayal of one's own country (7)
30 Author of *I, Claudius* (6,6)

DOWN

1 Hans ——, court painter to Henry VIII (7)
2 The eggs of lice (4)
3 Cricket balls bowled with speed direct to batsman's feet (7)
4 South American country with capital Montevideo (7)
5 Brilliant stratagem often associated with the sudden overthrow of a government (4)
6 Jan ——, one-time TV news reader (7)
7 Ontario, Erie, Huron, Michigan and Superior (3,5,5)
8 American astronaut who was the first man on the moon (4,9)
14 Great brilliance, conspicuous success or acclaim (5)
15 Mushrooms, toadstools etc (5)
19 Mimi's lover in *La Boheme* (7)
20 eg Argon, iodine or krypton (7)
21 Scale by which earthquakes are measured (7)
22 Greek goddess of retributive justice (7)
26 Fencing sword with a bowl shaped guard (4)
27 Diesel fuel (4)

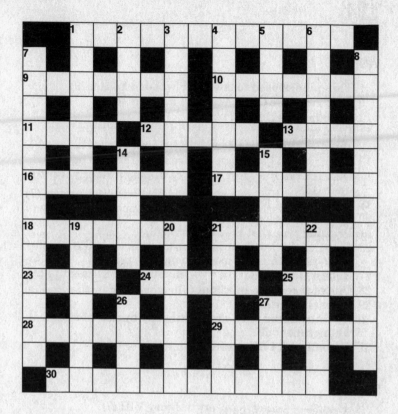

114

ACROSS

1 Thin planks used to cover US wooden houses (9)
9 Creator of the Great Western Railway (6)
10 US humorist (1902-71) (5,4)
11 Lapwing (6)
12 Bundles of fibrous tissue joining bones or cartilages (9)
13 A Semitic god to whom children were sacrificed (6)
17 District on the west coast of India, formerly Portuguese (3)
19 Conqueror of Everest (7)
20 Dismiss from a post in disgrace (7)
21 Printing type that is in a jumble (3)
23 "——, if the lower orders don't set us a good example, what on earth is the use of them?" (Wilde) (6)
27 Robert Dudley, Earl of ——, favourite of Elizabeth I (9)
28 One of three men in a boat (6)
29 Potassium nitrate (9)
30 He introduced the antiseptic treatment of surgical wounds (6)
31 A small white composite Alpine flower (9)

DOWN

2 A covered open arcade (6)
3 House made from standardised parts assembled on site (3-3)
4 Snow leopards (6)
5 Rice cooked in stock with meat & vegetables (7)
6 Pub that is not tied to a brewery (9)
7 National Park in Wales (9)
8 Makers of arrows (9)
14 British wartime leader (9)
15 Cause of *The Ancient Mariner*'s bad luck (9)
16 Chief official of district under Nazi regime (9)
17 Cambridge college servant (3)
18 Highest card (3)
22 Composer who set Masefield's *Sea Fever* to music (7)
24 Liquid formed by oxidation of alcohol (6)
25 Member of an ascetic Jewish sect in ancient Palestine (6)
26 Suit of cards (6)

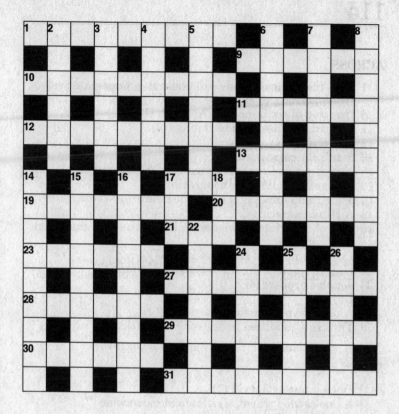

115

ACROSS

1 The theoretical study of control processes in electronic, mechanical and biological systems (11)
8 Any one of six Concertos by Bach (11)
11 Bird which flies high as it sings (4)
12 eg Victoria (4)
13 Small Balearic isle (7)
15 New York avenue synonymous with advertising (7)
16 Silk voile or other thin material (5)
17 Tube that conveys blood to the heart (4)
18 A Hindu ascetic (4)
19 One of two Hebrew leaders allowed to enter the Promised Land (5)
21 Previous name of Livorno, Italy (7)
22 Unit for measuring the intensity of sound (7)
23 Jacob's brother (4)
26 Dry (4)
27 Alternative name for Aberdeen (7,4)
28 The cross-mouthed fishes such as sharks and rays (11)

DOWN

2 Once know as Jorvik (4)
3 A one-seeded wheat, *Triticum monococcum* (7)
4 Christmas (4)
5 A lamaserai is a —— monastery (7)
6 Fish from the family *Cyprinidae* (4)
7 A drink of champagne and Guinness in equal parts (5,6)
8 Country of giants visited by Gulliver (11)
9 Where Joseph of Arimathea's staff took root and budded (11)
10 Medium, dry sherry—the subject of a tale by Edgar Allan Poe (11)
14 The first bishop at Lindisfarne (5)
15 Bicycle with a small engine (5)
19 A fortified island in a lake in either Scotland or Ireland (7)
20 Panda (4-3)
24 River which flows SW and S into the Caspian Sea (4)
25 Essential oil made from the damask rose (4)
26 It was split by Ernest Rutherford in 1919 (4)

116

ACROSS

1 This bay is a large inland sea in northern Canada (6)
4 Sir Henry —— , inventor of steel-making process (8)
8 Architectural style in W Europe from 12th to 16th century (6)
9 Tree with hanging yellow flowers (8)
10 Surpassed inimportance or power (8)
11 Humphry —— , English landscape gardener 1752-1818 (6)
12 Chess position in which one player can only move into a less advantageous position (8)
13 Mount where Noah's Ark came to rest (6)
15 Maria —— , Greek operatic soprano (6)
18 Food served in a small dish (8)
20 Transliteration of Modern Greek name for Euboea, Greece's second largest island (6)
21 Thick short double-breasted plaid coat in North America (8)
23 Circular tower for coastal defence (8)
24 Feeble-minded or senile person (6)
25 Talked idly and at length (8)
26 John —— , author of *Paradise Lost* (6)

DOWN

1 The —— , seat of government in the Netherlands (5)
2 Thin slice of veal (9)
3 Capital of Cyprus since 10th century (7)
4 Thriller written by Sapper (Herman Cyril McNeile) in 1920 (4-3,8)
5 Vast region of Russia and N Kazakhstan (7)
6 Large and frightening imaginary creature (7)
7 Philo —— , US inventor of typewriter and breech-loading rifle (9)
12 Solly —— , zoologist, chief scientific adviser to British government from 1964 to 1971 (9)
14 Judicial discharge (9)
16 Hare less than one year old (7)
17 Instrument for inserting wires into paper (7)
19 Tarmac road surface (7)
22 Foremost Anglo-Saxon deity (5)

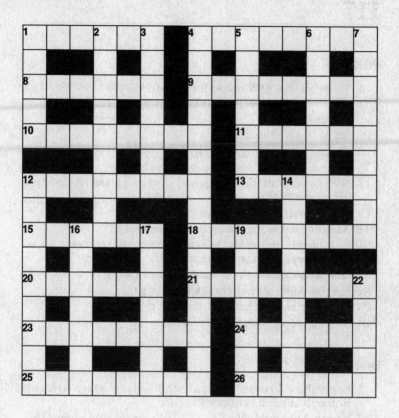

117

ACROSS

1 Town on the IOW noted for its regatta (5)
4 John —— , novelist whose works include *Paradise Postponed* (8)
8 Light-hearted satire (8)
9 Process of wearing down by friction (8)
11 Eighth month of the Roman calendar (7)
13 NW suburb of Los Angeles, centre of the American film industry (9)
15 Novel written by Jane Austen (10,5)
18 Another name for potassium nitrate (9)
21 —— acid, optically inactive form of tartaric acid sometimes found in grape juice (7)
22 One who refuses to do military service (8)
24 Person who catches things in a trap (8)
25 Banister used to provide support (8)
26 Search into books for information (5)

DOWN

1 Legendary Roman general who led an army against Rome in the 5th century BC (10)
2 James Abbott McNeill —— , US painter and etcher (8)
3 Shrub that grows in alkaline desert regions (8)
4 Hindu goddess of illusion (4)
5 Formal agreement between two or more states (6)
6 One of a breed of sheep valued for its fine wool (6)
7 Reddish-coloured horse (4)
10 *Daydream* ——, hit for the Monkees in 1967 (8)
12 Inflammation of the lining of the nose (8)
14 Richard —— —— , impresario noted for his productions of Gilbert & Sullivan operattas (5,5)
16 Class comprising spiders, scorpions etc (8)
17 Scottish castle, a royal residence (8)
19 Plant which grows on rocks, trees etc (6)
20 Fish which can inflate its body into a globe shape (6)
22 Nickname for Peterborough United's football team (4)
23 Swiss patriot who shot an apple from his son's head (4)

ACROSS

1 Another name for the aubergine (8)
9 Christina Georgina and Dante Gabriel, sister and brother poets (8)
10 Greek god of war (4)
11 Long wooden pole used in defence (12)
13 Continually given the same kind of role (8)
15 Distinguishing mark of social disgrace (6)
16 Conservative prime minister 1834-5 and 1841-6 (4)
17 Main division of a long poem (5)
18 German composer of the opera *Antigone* (4)
20 Capital of Northern Territory of Australia (6)
21 Of a spectacle lens having three sections (8)
23 Independent school near Godalming in Surrey (12)
26 River flowing into North Sea at Middlesborough (4)
27 Device for heating a room (8)
28 Aquatic, burrowing, egg-laying, Australian mammal (8)

DOWN

2 Projecting spout, usually grotesquely carved (8)
3 Anemone with bell-shaped purple blooms (6-6)
4 Capital of Turkey (6)
5 Moderately fast pace of a horse (4)
6 Form of coffee-making machine or the coffee so made (8)
7 Volcano in Sicily (4)
8 Undesirable common people (4-4)
12 Branch of mathematics dealing with relations between sides and angles of triangles (12)
14 Doctrine, dogma or belief (5)
16 Treatment of corns, bunions and other minor foot ailments (8)
17 Composition in sonata form for solo instruments and orchestra (8)
19 Burning or flaming torch (8)
22 Tropical American lizard (6)
24 Opera by Italian composer Giuseppe Verdi (4)
25 Musical instrument played by plucking strings (4)

119

ACROSS

1 Of an angelic being of the second order of the celestial hierarchy (8)
6 Upper part of a woman's dress (6)
9 Material used in resurfacing roads (6)
10 & 11 Duo with hit Lovers of the World Unite in 1966 (5,3,8)
11 See 10
12 Greek satirist noted for his Dialogues of the Gods (6)
13 Of Cambridge or Cambridge University (12)
16 Train driver or his assistant (12)
19 Lighthouse on an island in the Bay of Alexandria (6)
21 First king of the northern kingdom of Israel (Old Testament) (8)
23 Hawaiian dance performed by a woman (4-4)
24 He was the oldest and wisest of the Greeks in the Trojan War (6)
25 Tristan's partner in musical drama by Wagner (6)
26 Chain of islands in the West Indies (8)

DOWN

2 Type of collision in which the fronts collide (4-2)
3 Cuban dance, or ballroom dance derived from it (5)
4 Dance, song or revel in honour of the god of wine (9)
5 Outstanding virtuoso solo passage (7)
6 Tool for measuring angles that opens like a pair of compasses (5)
7 Plane figure with twelve sides and angles (9)
8 Vermilion-coloured sulphide of mercury (8)
13 Shriek that sounds like a cat on heat (9)
14 Dutch artist who painted some 60 self-portraits between 1629-1669 (9)
15 Riding breeches that are tight-fitting from thighs to ankles (8)
17 —— Taxi, hit by Herb Alpert in 1966 (7)
18 The early freeing of a prisoner on condition that he is of good behaviour (6)
20 Fry food quickly in a little fat (5)
22 Sybil Fawlty's husband (5)

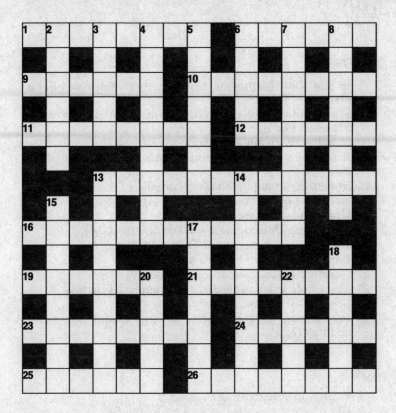

ACROSS

1 In the New Testament, the father of James and John (7)
5 Fine white linen originally manufactured in French Flanders (7)
9 Member of a wandering tribe (5)
10 Australian warbler or South American humming-bird (9)
11 Romantic drama by Shakespeare (3,7)
12 Architect of St Paul's Cathedral (4)
14 Unfavourable state of affairs (12)
18 He became Paul in the New Testament (4,2,6)
21 Uncle —— , character in *Tristram Shandy* (4)
22 Port and resort in East Kent (10)
25 Geometrical surface or solid object (9)
26 The whole when regarded as a complete sum (5)
27 *Seesaw,* —— *Daw*, nursery-rhyme (7)
28 Paramaribo is the capital of this South American country (7)

DOWN

1 Point opposite nadir (6)
2 Bar on car to lessen shock of collision (6)
3 Australian wind instrument (10)
4 Legal word meaning to hinder or prevent (5)
5 Point of transfer between two main railway lines (9)
6 Variety of cat without a tail (4)
7 Force person to do something with haste or by unfair means (8)
8 Pan with perforated bottom used for straining and rinsing (8)
13 Harsh questioner (10)
15 Collection of poems (9)
16 Temperature line on a map (8)
17 One who makes petty complaints or observations (8)
19 Largest city in New England, capital of Massachusetts (6)
20 Fine parchment prepared from animal skin (6)
23 Fame or renown (5)
24 John —— , English portrait and historical painter (4)

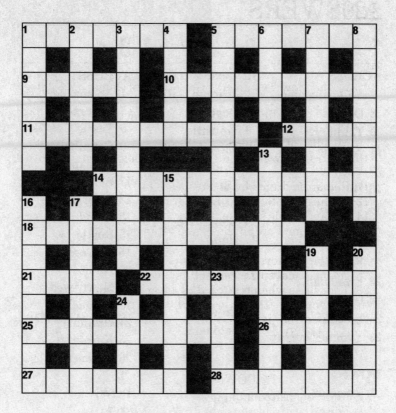

ANSWERS

1

ACROSS

1 Yellowhammer
8 Occlude
9 Tannery
11 Katrine
12 Purlieu
13 Hinge
14 Engulfing
16 Retinitis
19 Prahu
21 Falcula
23 Ewe-lamb
24 Gavotte
25 Epizoon
26 Yvonne Murray

DOWN

1 Yucatan
2 Leucite
3 Overexert
4 Het up
5 Mineral
6 Emeriti
7 Yorkshire fog
10 Younghusband
15 Gaspereau
17 Tel Aviv
18 Neuston
19 Premier
20 Anatomy
22 Abele

2

ACROSS

1 Jeannie C Riley
7 Depot
8 Sinusitis
9 Vitriol
10 Stadium
11 Larne
12 Allotment
14 Ennerdale
17 Hanif
19 Retreat
21 Tendril
22 Verdigris
23 Trews
24 Solomon Grundy

DOWN

1 Jupiter
2 Astride
3 Ennis
4 Restart
5 Latrine
6 Yosemite falls
7 Dave Lee Travis
8 Sultana
13 Laertes
15 Natural
16 Rhenium
17 Honiton
18 Nursery
20 Turin

3

ACROSS

1 Abomasum
5 Syntax
8 Tassie
9 Cannibal
10 Chickpea
11 Asleep
12 Squirrel
13 Pseudo
15 Rustic
18 Lacrosse
20 Number
21 Newly-wed
23 Binnacle
24 Hatpin
25 Karate
26 Sediment

DOWN

1 Aztec
2 Masochist
3 Sweeper
4 Michael Flanders
5 Syncarp
6 Tableau
7 Xylophone
12 Springbok
14 Ecosystem
16 Seminar
17 Coracle
19 Cowshed
22 Donut

4

ACROSS
1 Xyster
4 Larkspur
8 Balsam
9 Organism
10 Camellia
11 Luther
12 Stressed
13 Severn
15 Russet
18 Offshoot
20 Miasma
21 Solecism
23 Huguenot
24 Roller
25 Wheatear
26 Merlin

DOWN
1 Xebec
2 Tasteless
3 Romulus
4 Leonard Rossiter
5 Regulus
6 Prithee
7 Rembrandt
12 Scrimshaw
14 Vehicular
16 Spangle
17 Trainee
19 Fulcrum
22 Moron

5

ACROSS
1 Tibet
4 Critique
8 Aviatrix
9 Agitator
11 Jehovah
13 Immingham
15 Kenneth Williams
18 Razor-back
21 Yangtze
22 Turnpike
24 Demerara
25 Fraction
26 Setae

DOWN
1 Tear-jerker
2 Brighton
3 Titivate
4 Coxa
5 Tartan
6 Quitch
7 Ewer
10 Gimmicky
12 Highjack
14 Masquerade
16 Leanness
17 Abstract
19 Zareba
20 Report
22 Turf
23 Eden

6

ACROSS
1 Vade-mecum
6 Sprig
9 Singlet
10 Epaulette
11 Ocarina
12 Pig-iron
13 Harvest festival
18 Calcium
20 Malaria
22 Megahertz
23 Alveoli
24 Lardy
25 Kettering

DOWN
1 Visigoth
2 Dinosaur
3 Malawi
4 Catena
5 May-apple
6 Skylight
7 Raptor
8 Gideon
14 Epiphany
15 Tamarisk
16 Virtuosi
17 Liaising
18 Cymbal
19 Logger
20 Mozart
21 Louvre

7

ACROSS

1 Gloria Hunniford
9 Bravery
10 Cocteau
11 Isinglass
12 Smith
13 Lehmann
15 Avignon
17 Abraham
19 Reefers
21 Quoit
23 Red-carpet
25 Initial
26 Cedilla
27 Hundred Years War

DOWN

1 Gabriel
2 Okapi
3 Ideograph
4 Hay Wain
5 Nicosia
6 Incus
7 Obedience
8 Dauphin
14 Harrovian
16 Icelander
17 Asquith
18 Marbled
19 Radicle
20 Set fair
22 Trier
24 Pilaw

8

ACROSS

1 Goldcrest
9 Splosh
10 Termagant
11 Octant
12 Think-tank
13 Bypath
17 Ark
19 Heartbreak Hotel
20 Tay
21 Lading
25 Afrikaans
26 Mohawk
27 Quickstep
28 Likely
29 Stonechat

DOWN

2 Obeche
3 Domino
4 Righto
5 San Andreas fault
6 Apocrypha
7 Bonaparte
8 Whitehall
14 Philomela
15 Handshake
16 Stonewall
17 Art
18 Kay
22 Zircon
23 Parsec
24 Entera

9

ACROSS

1 Wicklow
5 Pegasus
9 Coleridge-Taylor
10 Inca
11 Swath
12 Beau
15 Ammeter
16 Apropos
17 Hoodlum
19 Mustang
21 Lath
22 Amide
23 Faro
26 Frances de la Tour
27 Ximenes
28 Khayyam

DOWN

1 Wichita
2 Cold Comfort Farm
3 Lory
4 Widower
5 Plectra
6 Gray
7 Self-explanatory
8 Strauss
13 Styli
14 Brest
17 Halifax
18 Mimesis
19 Midweek
20 Grogram
24 Icon
25 Java

10

ACROSS
1 Chromosome
6 Asia
9 Transplant
10 Brie
13 Bronchi
15 Keynes
16 United
17 Johnny Tillotson
18 Cognac
20 Sclera
21 Gavotte
22 Ivry
25 Pied-à-terre
26 Gust
27 Cornucopia

DOWN
1 City
2 Rial
3 Messrs
4 Silence is golden
5 Manchu
7 Strathspey
8 Aberdonian
11 Skyjacking
12 Pythagoras
13 Beanbag
14 Invoice
19 Calico
20 Static
23 Prep
24 Jena

11

ACROSS
1 Hercules
9 Apologia
10 Pear
11 Anna Karenina
13 Atlantic
15 Diwali
16 Isis
17 Cedar
18 Omsk
20 Corrie
21 Zaniness
23 Squirrel-tail
26 Acne
27 Overland
28 Aberdeen

DOWN
2 Emeritus
3 Caravanserai
4 Linnet
5 Sack
6 Corridor
7 Ugli
8 Tamarisk
12 Newfoundland
14 Cadiz
16 Incision
17 Clearway
19 Suspense
22 Nuance
24 Used
25 Leda

12

ACROSS
1 Solomon
5 Wine-sap
9 Hyson
10 Nonpareil
11 Stereotype
12 Slur
14 Pablo Picasso
18 Auld lang syne
21 Chow
22 Handicraft
25 Reichstag
26 Attar
27 Tweeter
28 Sitwell

DOWN
1 Schism
2 Lister
3 Monte Carlo
4 Nonet
5 Windpipes
6 Noah
7 Seedless
8 Poltroon
13 Iconoclast
15 Lancaster
16 Baccarat
17 Fluoride
19 Sartre
20 Sterol
23 Degas
24 Phut

13

ACROSS

1 Stay-at-home type
9 Lateral
10 Skirret
11 Sump
12 Gorgonzola
14 Arable
15 Endogamy
17 Premolar
18 Stroud
21 Crustacean
22 Agra
24 Fondant
25 Lumbago
26 Extinct volcano

DOWN

1 Silesia
2 Autumnal equinox
3 Aura
4 Helios
5 Misogyny
6 Teignmouth
7 Persona non grata
8 Steamy
13 Altostrati
16 Narcotic
17 Pacify
19 Diabolo
20 Pavlov
23 Amyl

14

ACROSS

8 Ephemera
9 Ithaca
10 Lar
11 Placenta
12 Croton
13 Gotterdammerung
15 Flummox
18 Pastern
21 Eternal triangle
24 Nilgai
25 Amaranth
26 Nun
27 Belloc
28 Trombone

DOWN

1 Apollo
2 Tercet
3 Leonardo da Vinci
4 Galahad
5 Circumnavigator
6 Theocrat
7 Schooner
14 Tau
16 Latticed
17 Marigold
19 Erg
20 Atlanta
22 Nearby
23 Lutine

15

ACROSS

6 The Two Ronnies
8 Amiens
9 Date-line
10 Tea
11 Scampi
12 Wedgwood
14 Anyroad
16 Kinloss
20 Dulcimer
23 Cumuli
24 Och
25 Cicatrix
26 Whammy
27 Good Samaritan

DOWN

1 Redeemer
2 Swastika
3 Bradawl
4 United
5 Willow
6 Time-consuming
7 Song of Solomon
13 Gin
15 Obi
17 Inch-worm
18 Lambaste
19 Proximo
21 Cracow
22 Morass

16

ACROSS
- **1** Aurora Australis
- **9** Redbreast
- **10** Churr
- **11** Nonsuch
- **12** Ecuador
- **13** Eil
- **14** Hurtled
- **17** Lateran
- **19** Gestapo
- **22** Jackdaw
- **24** Ecu
- **25** Tankard
- **26** Karachi
- **28** Infra
- **29** Publicist
- **30** Golden saxifrage

DOWN
- **1** Air on the G string
- **2** Rodin
- **3** Rorqual
- **4** Abashed
- **5** Sitwell
- **6** Racquet
- **7** Laundered
- **8** Sir Frank Whittle
- **15** Resentful
- **16** Esp
- **18** Aga
- **20** Anatase
- **21** Oedipus
- **22** Juke-box
- **23** Cardiff
- **27** China

17

ACROSS
- **1** Trial By Jury
- **10** Payee
- **11** Worthless
- **12** Tellurium
- **13** Uriah
- **14** Arroyo
- **16** Majestic
- **18** Minehead
- **20** Crambo
- **23** Lehar
- **24** Slingshot
- **26** Germinate
- **27** Mardi
- **28** Deuteronomy

DOWN
- **2** Royal
- **3** Avebury
- **4** Bewail
- **5** Jeremiad
- **6** Rehouse
- **7** Ophthalmology
- **8** Seriatim
- **9** Eschscholtzia
- **15** Ranchero
- **17** Camshaft
- **19** Hircine
- **21** Regimen
- **22** Linear
- **25** Hiram

18

ACROSS
- **1** Agatha Christie
- **9** Freeze-up
- **10** Owner
- **12** Elbe
- **13** Shish kebab
- **15** Literary
- **16** Revere
- **18** Wretch
- **20** Undersea
- **23** Tarantella
- **24** Gobi
- **26** Niche
- **27** Inscribe
- **28** Nebuchadnezzar

DOWN
- **2** Acrobat
- **3** Heel
- **4** Cheshire
- **5** Repast
- **6** Shopkeeper
- **7** Ignoble
- **8** Problematic
- **11** Yellowstone
- **14** Fricandeau
- **17** Analysed
- **19** Earache
- **21** Showbiz
- **22** Fetish
- **25** Brie

19

ACROSS
1 Constrictor
9 Unco
10 Audiometric
11 Slav
14 Nabokov
16 Tel Aviv
17 Vexed
18 Root
19 Emma
20 Cream
22 Timothy
23 Nominal
24 Tell
28 Christendom
29 Duty
30 Evasiveness

DOWN
2 Ovum
3 Spiv
4 Romanov
5 Cote
6 Omitted
7 Enslavement
8 Convivially
12 Ingratitude
13 Abnormality
15 Veery
16 Texan
20 Chekhov
21 Molotov
25 Diss
26 Anon
27 Moss

20

ACROSS
1 Black Forest
8 Prickly-pear
11 Leek
12 Tong
13 Veering
15 Scanner
16 Erica
17 Ross
18 Byng
19 Overt
21 Wallaby
22 Ferment
23 Slip
26 Peso
27 Stegosaurus
28 Traditional

DOWN
2 Lurk
3 Cocaine
4 Folk
5 Replica
6 Spat
7 Oliver Twist
8 Peter Sallis
9 Rodney Bewes
10 Aggregation
14 Gravy
15 Scurf
19 Obliged
20 Testudo
24 Pter
25 Psst
26 Puma

21

ACROSS
1 Johannesburg
8 Tamarin
9 Antwerp
11 Laid out
12 Dottier
13 Elate
14 Edinburgh
16 Bethlehem
19 Velar
21 Sanctum
23 Risotto
24 Harpist
25 Itchier
26 Bloemfontein

DOWN
1 Jamaica
2 Hormone
3 Ninetieth
4 Eland
5 Bathtub
6 Reedier
7 Stellenbosch
10 Port Harcourt
15 Immersion
17 Tendril
18 Lattice
19 Vesicle
20 Lothian
22 Motif

22

ACROSS
1 Pegasus
5 Pelican
9 Minim
10 Radiogram
11 Chronology
12 Pitt
14 Merry-go-round
18 Garden of Eden
21 Racy
22 Prejudiced
25 Goldfinch
26 Heads
27 Retrace
28 Diploma

DOWN
1 Pumice
2 Gantry
3 Simon Peter
4 Sural
5 Pedagogue
6 Laos
7 Curlicue
8 Nematode
13 Friendship
15 Rio Grande
16 Agar-agar
17 Bracelet
19 Octavo
20 Odessa
23 Jihad
24 Offa

23

ACROSS
1 Gethsemane
6 Scut
9 Marionette
10 Lear
12 Lunacy
13 Jodhpurs
15 Sweet-William
18 Reprimanding
21 Parakeet
22 Whoosh
24 Saga
25 Ironmonger
26 Lope
27 Unladylike

DOWN
1 Gamble
2 Tyrone
3 Scotch whisky
4 Mien
5 Nationwide
7 Cherubim
8 Tiresome
11 Philanthropy
14 Decahedron
16 Proposal
17 Spark-gap
19 Mowgli
20 Charge
23 Anna

24

ACROSS
1 H G Wells
5 Abscess
9 Begonia
10 Opossum
11 Tiara
12 A P Herbert
13 Siemens
14 Romania
16 P W Botha
19 Roll-top
22 Jurywoman
24 One-up
25 Medical
26 Vertigo
27 Someone
28 Re-entry

DOWN
1 H E Bates
2 W G Grace
3 Lineament
4 Sea-bass
5 A N Other
6 Stour
7 Eastern
8 Sumatra
15 Melbourne
16 P D James
17 Boredom
18 A A Milne
19 Run over
20 T S Eliot
21 P J Proby
23 Wacko

25

ACROSS
1 Yorick
4 Chinaman
9 Maoist
10 Spartans
12 31 & 26 Mies van der Rohe
13 Chloe
14 Bohr
17 Trinity House
20 Chromaticity
23 Olav
24 Argus
25 Edda
28 Arbroath
29 Ostend
30 Clarence
31 See **12**

DOWN
1 Yamamoto
2 Rhodesia
3 Cosa
5 Hippopotamus
6 Nero
7 Meadow
8 Nostra
11 Chrysocratic
15 Bight
16 Asdic
18 Bindweed
19 Lysander
21 Mosaic
22 Zambia
26 See **12**
27 Asia

26

ACROSS
1 Republican
6 Moab
10 Monet
11 Innocents
12 Ignatius
13 Iceni
15 Marxism
17 Alberta
19 Toccata
21 Panache
22 Fugue
24 De loyola
27 Excalibur
28 Liege
29 Dhow
30 Leominster

DOWN
1 Rump
2 Panegyric
3 Botha
4 Iridium
5 Amnesia
7 Ounce
8 Bastinated
9 Scriabin
14 Smithfield
16 Isabella
18 Recollect
20 Audible
21 Pilgrim
23 Gecko
25 Yulan
26 Lear

27

ACROSS
8 Asphyxia
9 Annexe
10 Rod
11 Dihedron
12 Asimov
13 Birds of a feather
15 Joy-ride
18 Luddite
21 Wells-next-the-sea
24 Elixir
25 Larkspur
26 Ido
27 Darnel
28 Talented

DOWN
1 Assisi
2 Shield
3 Extraordinarily
4 Farnham
5 Madame Butterfly
6 Anointed
7 Exponent
14 Ray
16 Overleaf
17 Relaxant
19 Its
20 Axolotl
22 Essene
23 Exuded

28

ACROSS

1 Gonorrhoea
6 Prop
10 Moped
11 Laplander
12 Transept
13 Doric
15 Ottoman
17 Yucatan
19 Kashmir
21 Cheetah
22 Brava
24 Manacles
27 Rabbinate
28 Nieve
29 Acts
30 Pentahedra

DOWN

1 Game
2 Nephritis
3 Rodin
4 Holbein
5 Empathy
7 Radar
8 Pyracantha
9 Sadducee
14 Kookaburra
16 Mammalia
18 Title deed
20 Rampage
21 Contest
23 Abbot
25 Conch
26 Mesa

29

ACROSS

1 Abstract art
8 Jam tomorrow
11 Mope
12 Kora
13 Powdery
15 Caulked
16 Kelly
17 Nile
18 Cash
19 Trent
21 Frinton
22 Grouser
23 Rome
26 Tile
27 Spinning top
28 Sagittarius

DOWN

2 Brae
3 Titlark
4 Alma
5 Torquay
6 Rook
7 H M S Pinafore
8 J P R Williams
9 Workmanship
10 Card-sharper
14 Yearn
15 Cling
19 Tournai
20 Trigger
24 Epha
25 Kilt
26 Tofu

30

ACROSS

1 Bridgewater
10 Imply
11 Swordfish
12 Derring-do
13 Woden
14 Rommel
16 Giordano
18 Iron duke
20 Bardic
23 Sugar
24 The Fellow
26 Entrechat
27 Imago
28 Alison Moyet

DOWN

2 Roper
3 Daytime
4 Ensign
5 Apologia
6 Endower
7 Kidderminster
8 Windward
9 Thane of Cawdor
15 Moorgate
17 Sketches
19 Durrell
21 Amerigo
22 Beaton
25 Lease

31

ACROSS

1 New Hebrides
7 Quoit
8 Jack-Straw
10 Apology
11 Princes
12 Twist
13 Biorhythm
16 Remittent
18 Ammon
19 Emperor
22 Harslet
23 Kidnapped
24 Caper
25 Greenmantle

DOWN

1 Neologism
2 Without
3 Enjoyable
4 Recap
5 Distich
6 Serac
7 Quarter-deck
9 Westminster
14 Octahedra
15 Time-lapse
17 Terrace
18 Apricot
20 Pi-dog
21 Ripon

32

ACROSS

1 Buchan
4 Appendix
9 & 3 Nitric Acid
10 Stirrups
12 Fall
13 Snark
14 Blue
17 Counterpoint
20 Hampton Court
23 Et al
24 *See 27*
25 Skua
28 Idomeneo
29 Bireme
30 *See 7*
31 Hellas

DOWN

1 Boniface
2 Catullus
3 *See 9*
5 Peterborough
6 Ezra
7 & 30 Double
  Entendre
8 Xyster
11 Entrepreneur
15 Straw
16 Knock
18 Tuckwell
19 Steamers
21 Belize
22 Ragout
26 Penn
27 & 24 Mike Leigh

33

ACROSS

4 Sheridan
8 Eczema
9 Airedale
10 Crucifer
11 Seamer
12 Cinerama
13 Neap tide
16 Dynamics
19 Thatcher
21 Impale
23 Ischemia
24 Flip-flop
25 Diadem
26 Wall-eyes

DOWN

1 Scorpio
2 Leukaemia
3 Raffia
4 Stars and
  Stripes
5 Etruscan
6 India
7 Allseed
14 Thackeray
15 Pipeclay
17 Yamulka
18 Decibel
20 Arcady
22 Ampul

34

ACROSS

1 Kilimanjaro
7 Noctuid
8 Two-step
10 Troth
11 Scapegoat
12 Isfahan
14 Leander
15 Gremlin
18 Sidecar
20 Ecosystem
21 Scrim
22 Spinoza
23 Tetanus
24 Middlemarch

DOWN

1 Kick-off
2 Louth
3 Madison
4 Netball
5 Aforesaid
6 Outsold
7 Nothingness
9 Peter grimes
13 Hollywood
16 Egotism
17 Nutgall
18 Symptom
19 Corinth
21 Satyr

35

ACROSS

1 Nebuchadnezzar
9 Saraband
10 Ozone
12 Elmo
13 Stereotype
15 Aznavour
16 Big end
18 Squire
20 Organism
23 Accordions
24 Asti
26 Chloe
27 Solarium
28 Constantinople

DOWN

2 Brahmin
3 Chad
4 Acanthus
5 Nadirs
6 Zoological
7 Anodyne
8 Legerdemain
11 Renaissance
14 Evergreens
17 Frontlet
19 Uccello
21 Insculp
22 Fiesta
25 Cran

36

ACROSS

1 Redgauntlet
10 Algol
11 Trousseau
12 Ectomorph
13 Lemur
14 Fleche
16 Beanpole
18 Rigorous
20 Winkle
23 Wales
24 Oversight
26 Syndicate
27 Durer
28 Silas Marner

DOWN

2 Ergot
3 Galumph
4 Upturn
5 Trochlea
6 Epsilon
7 Haverfordwest
8 Teamwork
9 Fuerteventura
15 Egg-plant
17 Automata
19 Rossini
21 Insider
22 Redeem
25 Gorse

37

ACROSS
1 Dr Zhivago
9 Cicada
10 Godmother
11 Acacia
12 Nectarine
13 Nausea
17 Aha
19 Frenchman's Creek
20 Pry
21 Rookie
25 Greenland
26 Ashets
27 Buccaneer
28 Debark
29 Desdemona

DOWN
2 Rhodes
3 Hamite
4 Votary
5 Green Chartreuse
6 Mischance
7 Lancaster
8 Balalaika
14 Sforzando
15 Xenophobe
16 Scripture
17 Amp
18 Any
22 Fenced
23 Plenum
24 Unseen

38

ACROSS
1 Quiller-Couch
8 Akabusi
9 Antonym
11 Bossism
12 Adam Ant
13 Twang
14 Tightrope
16 Almsgiver
19 Sabot
21 Regalia
23 All over
24 Nearest
25 Humerus
26 Pennsylvania

DOWN
1 Quassia
2 Inuring
3 Leitmotiv
4 Riata or Reata
5 Outcast
6 Centavo
7 Rabbit-warren
10 Mother Teresa
15 Gorbachov or Gorbachev
17 Magnate
18 Galleon
19 Solomon
20 Bavaria
22 Aptly

39

ACROSS
1 Santa Cruz
9 Exotica
10 Stamina
11 Hessian
12 Speakeasy
14 Princess
15 Byssus
17 Ptolemy
20 Aether
23 Burnouse
25 Wristband
26 Canasta
27 Lullaby
28 Lambeth
29 Equerries

DOWN
2 Autopsy
3 Tomcats
4 Canoeist
5 Zephyr
6 Ross-on-Wye
7 Miniver
8 Bannister
13 Speller
15 Benbecula
16 Upholster
18 Masseuse
19 Grandma
21 Tubular
22 Ennoble
24 Swathe

40

ACROSS

1 Seraph
4 Istanbul
10 Longitude
11 Grieg
12 Brocade
13 Pennant
14 Ranee
15 Finchley
18 Catacomb
20 Robot
23 Iranian
25 Avignon
26 Drill
27 Astronaut
28 Windmill
29 & 22 Leaded
   Window

DOWN

1 Salzburg
2 Rangoon
3 Primavera
5 Sleeping Beauty
6 Argon
7 Brigade
8 Legato
9 Duke of
   Cornwall
16 Herbivore
17 Stansted
19 Arabian
21 Bonnard
22 See 29
24 Islam

41

ACROSS

1 Hermit-crab
6 Marc
9 Wavelenght
10 Brie
12 Icebox
13 Schemata
15 Stradivarius
18 Extravaganza
21 Westerly
22 Pedalo
24 Rome
25 Sneezewort
26 Hank
27 Mauritania

DOWN

1 Hawaii
2 Review
3 Isle of Thanet
4 Cane
5 Anticlimax
7 Adriatic
8 Crevasse
11 Bedazzlement
14 Casablanca
16 Bedworth
17 Stasimon
19 Baboon
20 Portia
23 Wear

42

ACROSS

7 Equerry
8 Greaves
10 Sidelights
11 Paul
12 Pericarp
14 Attica
15 Psychedelia
19 Paella
20 Devonian
22 Puce
23 Palindrome
25 Proctor
26 Darling

DOWN

1 Aquifer
2 Mede
3 Eroica
4 Dressage
5 Carpathian
6 Verucca
9 Chippendale
13 Insolvency
16 Champion
17 January
18 Hammond
21 Vandal
24 Rill

43

ACROSS

7 Churchill
8 Dewar
10 Frontier
11 Ashlar
12 Cowl
13 Artesian
15 Pandora
17 Ziganka
20 Literati
22 Test
25 Taylor
26 Cardamom
27 Adobe
28 Cleo Laine

DOWN

1 Shore
2 Franco
3 Thriller
4 Floreat
5 Bethesda
6 Balalaika
9 Cant
14 Garibaldi
16 Djellaba
18 Interpol
19 Lincoln
21 Agra
23 Scarab
24 Colne

44

ACROSS

7 Angostura
8 Aside
10 Baroness
11 Carter
12 Sage
13 Etruscan
15 Wolfram
17 Lanolin
20 Pomander
22 Gula
25 Falcon
26 Chipmunk
27 Torme
28 Palladium

DOWN

1 Snead
2 Corona
3 St Helena
4 Dresden
5 Espresso
6 Adrenalin
9 Acer
14 Sotomayor
16 Francome
18 Anguilla
19 Trucial
21 Dune
23 Lambda
24 Snout

45

ACROSS

7 Riviera
8 Cedilla
10 Chihuahuas
11 Hugh
12 Armagnac
14 Rialto
15 Hebephrenia
19 Zombie
20 Urbanity
22 Sofi
23 Abercromby
25 Malaria
26 Managua

DOWN

1 Richard
2 Sikh
3 Ordain
4 Tesserae
5 Lithuanian
6 Blighty
9 Munchhausen
13 Azerbaijan
16 Elevatio
17 Potomac
18 Stibium
21 Buchan
24 Olaf

46

ACROSS

7 Starboard
8 Rodin
10 Tapeworm
11 Mastic
12 Ayes
13 Duodenum
15 Formosa
17 St Lucia
20 Man-of-war
22 Ipso
25 Taylor
26 Castries
27 Sting
28 Caribbean

DOWN

1 Stoat
2 Artery
3 Colossus
4 Bromide
5 Rousseau
6 Bilirubin
9 Umbo
14 Bonaparte
16 Moorland
18 Tailspin
19 Crucial
21 Ward
23 Strobe
24 Sedan

47

ACROSS

1 Andromache
6 Omsk
9 Silverside
10 Clod
12 Cravat
13 See 1 down
15 Clothes-horse
18 Carbohydrate
21 Monarchy
22 Scurvy
24 Tahr
25 Silhouette
26 Rose
27 Cerebellum

DOWN

1 & 13 Alsace Lorraine
2 Dallas
3 Open All Hours
4 Apse
5 Hydrometry
7 Milliard
8 Kedgeree
11 Architecture
14 Strychnine
16 Scimitar
17 Bronchus
19 Gretel
20 Lyceum
23 Ghee

48

ACROSS

1 Gran Canaria
10 Aruba
11 Bigarreau
12 Lanzarote
13 Nadir
14 Nectar
16 Tenerife
18 Intaglio
20 Scheme
23 Lundy
24 South Uist
26 North Uist
27 Baler
28 Inclination

DOWN

2 Rouen
3 Niagara
4 Albion
5 Anglesey
6 In range
7 Hayling Island
8 Headline
9 Fuerteventura
15 Catenary
17 Pigswill
19 Gryphon
21 Cohabit
22 Sultan
25 Igloo

49

ACROSS
1 Forget-me-not
9 Amphibian
10 Beech
11 Trojan
12 Betel-nut
13 Foster
15 Tartuffe
18 Southpaw
19 Cherub
21 Enduring
23 Stir up
26 Harsh
27 Campanili
28 Bittersweet

DOWN
1 & 18 Feast of Stephen
2 Repro
3 Elizabeth
4 Muir
5 Non-metal
6 Table
7 & 20 John the Baptist
8 Jennifer
14 Saunders
16 Tahitians
17 Wainscot
18 *See 1 down*
20 *See 7*
22 Rahab
24 Rhine
25 Smee

50

ACROSS
1 Wellingtonia
8 Algebra
9 Whitlow
11 Horatio
12 Slavery
13 Nadir
14 Acquiesce
16 Tarantara
19 Secco
21 Naphtha
23 Request
24 Cesspit
25 Thomson
26 Wendy Richard

DOWN
1 Wagered
2 Lobster
3 Inamorata
4 Gowns
5 Origami
6 Illness
7 Washington DC
10 Wayne Fontana
15 Quadratic
17 Riposte
18 Note-pad
19 Sequoia
20 Creased
22 Astor

51

ACROSS
1 Cheapskate
6 Skye
9 Chauvinist
10 Visa
13 Molotov
15 Asimov
16 Nougat
17 Jack-in-the-pulpit
18 Nippon
20 Ostend
21 Retouch
22 Runt
25 Power-lathe
26 Mayo
27 Fictitious

DOWN
1 Cock
2 Edam
3 Pavlov
4 King of the forest
5 Teston
7 Kriegspiel
8 Exactitude
11 Panjandrum
12 Pinchpenny
13 Monitor
14 Voguish
19 Neroli
20 Ocelot
23 Otto
24 Zeus

52

ACROSS

1 Smoke-bomb
9 Acronym
10 Screech
11 Berlioz
12 Palliasse
14 & 15 Platinum Blonde
15 *See 14*
17 Electro
20 Insect
23 Ranchero
25 Ursa Major
26 Malcolm
27 Goodwin
28 Russell
29 Edinburgh

DOWN

2 & 15 Michael Barrymore
3 Kremlin
4 Bechamel
5 Barbel
6 Proration
7 Indiana
8 Amazement
13 Spector
15 *See 2*
16 Dethroned
18 Rigadoon
19 Analyst
21 Spandau
22 Cooling
24 Rumble

53

ACROSS

1 Yachtswoman
7 Yahoo
8 Congruity
10 Ugandan
11 Spondyl
12 Naevi
13 Quasimodo
16 Woolliest
18 Minsk
19 Homonym
22 Colibri
23 Trattoria
24 Chute
25 Yackety-yack

DOWN

1 Yo-heave-ho
2 Chondri
3 Technique
4 Winds
5 Marconi
6 Naiad
7 You-know-what
9 Yellowknife
14 Autocracy
15 Osnabruck
17 Lunatic
18 Malacca
20 Mealy
21 Maree

54

ACROSS

1 Walthamstow
7 Whitsun
8 Glasgow
10 Limit
11 Yaroslavl
12 Ionized
14 Bradley
15 Missing
18 Raleigh
20 Orangeman
21 Visit
22 Yorkist
23 Walloon
24 Wensleydale

DOWN

1 Whitman
2 Liszt
3 Honeyed
4 Maghreb
5 Transvaal
6 Wagtail
7 William Cody
9 Wally Whyton
13 Zwinglian
16 Sparrow
17 Gametal
18 Ringway
19 Inshore
21 Villa

55

ACROSS

1 Morass
4 & 10 Henry the Navigator
10 *See 4*
11 Femme
12 Gunroom
13 Ypsilon
14 Amati
15 Orangery
18 Shiedam
20 Lathi
23 Pasteur
25 Tangier
26 & 27 Eliza Doolittle
27 *See 26*
28 Pan-pipes
29 Yemeni

DOWN

1 Monaghan
2 Ravenna
3 Signorini
5 Early day motion
6 Rufus
7 Templar
8 Exeunt
9 Stamford Bridge
16 Galantine
17 Disraeli
19 Caspian
21 Thistle
22 Upkeep
24 E-la-mi

56

ACROSS

1 Capsized
9 Aardwolf
10 Etui
11 Razzle-dazzle
13 Malinger
15 Rookie
16 Snag
17 Canon
18 Haft
20 Baboon
21 Windmill
23 Offscourings
26 Twig
27 Norseman
28 Glorying

DOWN

2 Autobahn
3 Stirling Moss
4 Zigzag
5 Dail
6 Gridiron
7 Boaz
8 Efferent
12 Zoochemistry
14 Renew
16 Subpoena
17 Consomme
19 Falchion
22 Nuncio
24 Farm
25 Rung

57

ACROSS

1 Sheraton
6 Bisect
9 Clotho
10 Mosquito
11 Quirinus
12 Awhile
13 Gainsborough
16 Ronnie Hilton
19 So long
21 Ethiopia
23 Quadrant
24 Dainty
25 Quarto
26 Aramaean

DOWN

2 Helium
3 Rotor
4 Thorndike
5 Nemesis
6 Basra
7 Southdown
8 Cytology
13 Gunpowder
14 Octahedra
15 Honolulu
17 Inertia
18 Sistra
20 Guano
22 Ouida

58

ACROSS

1 Zatopek
5 Zermatt
9 Rarer
10 Raptorial
11 Cavalryman
12 Lent
14 Experimental
18 Stratosphere
21 Ouse
22 Bluejacket
25 Bobsleigh
26 Dutch
27 Corinth
28 Rancher

DOWN

1 Zurich
2 Thrive
3 Perplexity
4 Kerry
5 Zephaniah
6 Rood
7 Anisette
8 Telltale
13 Bear-garden
15 Eastleigh
16 Ascorbic
17 Crossbar
19 Sketch
20 Etcher
23 Ether
24 Flan

59

ACROSS

1 John Wesley
6 Flab
9 Jocularity
10 Opah
12 Bulbul
13 Emporium
15 Swindle-sheet
18 Cardiologist
21 Irishism
22 Hebron
24 & 25 Life
   Expectancy
25 See 24
26 Silk
27 Unladylike

DOWN

1 Jujube
2 Heckle
3 Wilbur Wright
4 Sark
5 Entomology
7 Lopsided
8 Behemoth
11 Consistently
14 Anglo-Saxon
16 Achilles
17 Fruitful
19 Brunei
20 Enzyme
23 Lena

60

ACROSS

1 Razzmatazz
6 Howe
9 Epistolary
10 Mead
13 Kiloton
15 Rhinal
16 Nestor
17 Wish you were
   here
18 Renoir
20 Vigour
21 Devizes
22 Dunk
25 Similitude
26 Epee
27 Chesterton

DOWN

1 Rhea
2 Zoic
3 Methil
4 Tale of Two
   Cities
5 Zircon
7 Over-the-top
8 Elderberry
11 Trowbridge
12 Dissonance
13 Katydid
14 Nemesis
19 Relish
20 Venice
23 Just
24 Jean

61

ACROSS
1 Betelgeuse
6 Ibis
10 Doyen
11 Oestrogen
12 Hen-coop
13 Insculp
14 Adder's-tongue
18 Appurtenance
21 One-eyed
23 Pharaoh
24 Sacristan
25 Nepal
26 Lett
27 Correlated

DOWN
1 Buddha
2 Trying
3 Londonderry Air
4 Ecosphere
5 Sushi
7 Begrudge
8 Synopses
9 Bristol Channel
15 Sharpener
16 Carousel
17 Uppercut
19 Rajput
20 Whiled
22 Ditto

62

ACROSS
1 Rhesus
5 Tiberius
9 Filibuster
10 Myth
11 Quadrans
12 Layman
13 Ifni
15 Nematode
18 Quartier
19 Surd
21 Armagh
23 Nuthatch
25 Opec
26 Jack Horner
27 Arcturus
28 Dexter

DOWN
2 Haiku
3 Spin-drier
4 Squeak
5 Titus Andronicus
6 Bird-lime
7 Rummy
8 Uitlander
14 Fluorspar
16 Testatrix
17 Nightjar
20 Etched
22 Ascot
24 Crete

63

ACROSS
1 Lorna Doone
6 Abut
9 Vibex
10 Solitaire
12 Chandrasekhar
14 Ranchman
15 Alumna
17 Whoopi
19 Base-line
21 Shoulder-blade
24 Inspector
25 Ukase
26 Teme
27 Armageddon

DOWN
1 Lava
2 Rubicon
3 Aix-la-Chapelle
4 Obsidian
5 Nulla
7 Brixham
8 Tie-breaker
11 The Blue Danube
13 Brownshirt
16 Canberra
18 Opossum
20 Iceland
22 Ester
23 Penn

64

ACROSS

4 Dogsbody
8 Azalea
9 Wizardry
10 Umbrella
11 Aplomb
12 Standard
13 Inhumane
16 Mainland
19 Yarmouth
21 Orford
23 Importer
24 Thailand
25 Remake
26 Smeltery

DOWN

1 Azimuth
2 Clarendon
3 Paella
4 Do wah diddy diddy
5 Gazpacho
6 Beryl
7 Duramen
14 Melodrama
15 Mandrake
17 Abraham
18 Streaky
20 Rupert
22 Oriel

65

ACROSS

8 Allegory
9 Earwig
10 Opt
11 Intercom
12 Usurer
13 Three Men in a Boat
15 Ajaccio
18 Offside
21 Paris Symphonies
24 Poncho
25 Gujarati
26 Nog
27 Estate
28 Lodestar

DOWN

1 Plinth
2 Serene
3 Non-commissioned
4 Wyoming
5 Return of the Jedi
6 Arquebus
7 Vineyard
14 Ria
16 Jealousy
17 Chitchat
19 Idi
20 Smuggle
22 Nernst
23 Entrap

66

ACROSS

6 Rule Britannia
8 Uganda
9 Berliner
10 Toe
11 Delphi
12 Confetti
14 Platina
16 Salsify
20 Spare rib
23 Remedy
24 Ted
25 Salvador
26 Warble
27 The Gondoliers

DOWN

1 Plant-pot
2 Oblation
3 Wisbech
4 Macron
5 Endive
6 Rogue-elephant
7 Adeste fideles
13 Fal
15 Ice
17 Aardwolf
18 Somerset
19 Obtrude
21 Review
22 Radnor

67

ACROSS

1 Memsahib
5 Danzig
8 Norden
9 Bob Dylan
10 Keelhaul
11 Rapier
12 Cambodia
13 Hornet
15 Verger
18 Defector
20 Novena
21 Queen Mab
23 Ironside
24 Idiocy
25 Height
26 Kohinoor

DOWN

1 Minsk
2 Saddlebag
3 Hansard
4 Bubble and squeak
5 Deborah
6 Zillion
7 Generator
12 Cavendish
14 Recension
16 Ravioli
17 Realist
19 Flemish
22 Buyer

68

ACROSS

1 Withdrawal
6 Bess
9 Cynic
10 Scrimshaw
12 Grossglockner
14 Emanated
15 Mealie
17 Insult
19 Reminder
21 Undergraduate
24 Relief-map
25 Opium
26 X-ray
27 Star-bright

DOWN

1 Wick
2 Tanagra
3 Doctor at Large
4 Assessed
5 April
7 Ethanol
8 Sowerberry
11 My Cherie Amour
13 Oedipus Rex
16 Feldspar
18 Sedilia
20 Deeping
22 Remit
23 Smut

69

ACROSS

1 Happiness
8 Spiny anteater
11 Phlox
12 Admix
13 Satyr
16 Rattan
17 Eggnog
18 Omega
19 Tenuto
20 Durham
21 Knave
24 Shawm
26 Coypu
27 Geiger counter
28 Catamaran

DOWN

2 Annex
3 Piazza
4 Notary
5 Scapa
6 Appleton layer
7 Desmond Haynes
9 Spiritoso
10 Exogamous
13 Snook
14 Theta
15 Reade
22 Nutria
23 Verona
25 Magma
26 Canna

70

ACROSS

1 Little John
6 Ossa
10 Gabon
12 Abidjan
13 Anaemia
14 Whole-hearted
18 Marksmanship
21 Cajoled
22 Valentine
23 Obadiah
24 Indweller
25 Ionic
26 Ghee
27 Salmagundi

DOWN

1 Log-jam
2 Tabriz
3 Long John Silver
4 Juvenilia
5 Halma
7 Shipmate
8 Adelaide
9 Incapacitating
15 Histogram
16 Smocking
17 Prejudge
19 Finnan
20 Chi-chi
22 Delta

71

ACROSS

1 Jehoshaphat
7 Kintail
8 Hilltop
10 Nappy
11 Chameleon
12 Atropin
14 Tally-ho
15 Outsold
18 Amnesia
20 Realistic
21 Coomb
22 Tunisia
23 Soapbox
24 Rosencrantz

DOWN

1 Juniper
2 Heavy
3 Silicon
4 Athwart
5 Helvellyn
6 Tottery
7 Kangaroo-rat
9 Pandora's box
13 Psoriasis
16 Trainer
17 Detrain
18 Accuser
19 Showbiz
21 Chain

72

ACROSS

1 Socrates
9 Universe
10 Fisc
11 Kingsley Amis
13 Sting-ray
15 Callao
16 Alph
17 Homer
18 Aide
20 Rubric
21 Nickname
23 Peter Sellers
26 Dhow
27 Cashmere
28 Rallying

DOWN

2 Oriental
3 Rocking-horse
4 Turner
5 Suss
6 Silencer
7 Dram
8 Pershore
12 All Saints Day
14 Yemen
16 Airspace
17 Huckster
19 Demijohn
22 Crewel
24 Tess
25 Leer

73

ACROSS

1 Whinchat
6 Samuel
9 Ibidem
10 Bully-off
11 Polyglot
12 Miller
13 Fly on the wall
16 Impersonator
19 Friary
21 Wrestler
23 Isotherm
24 Tomato
25 Fag-end
26 Notation

DOWN

2 Hobson
3 Noddy
4 Himalayas
5 Tibetan
6 Salem
7 Mayflower
8 Enfeeble
13 Fremantle
14 Hottentot
15 Ambrosia
17 Newsman
18 Gentoo
20 Yield
22 Tempt

74

ACROSS

1 William Tell
7 Pests
8 Narcotism
10 Amorous
11 Trudeau
12 Taste
13 Represent
16 Genuflect
18 Mhorr
19 Nucleus
22 Itchier
23 Triumviri
24 Eliot
25 Sandringham

DOWN

1 Wisconsin
2 Lissome
3 Innisfree
4 Merit
5 Evolute
6 Loire
7 Plantagenet
9 Mount Ararat
14 Patrician
15 Eroticism
17 Freeman
18 Macbeth
20 Chips
21 Skier

75

ACROSS

1 Bahamas
5 Caracal
9 Tabular
10 Reverso
11 Natty
12 Cavalcade
13 Catalan
14 Nacarat
16 Road-map
19 Send-off
22 Maharajah
24 Altar
25 Diagram
26 Rustled
27 Nettles
28 Caraway

DOWN

1 Botanic
2 Habitat
3 Malayalam
4 Saracen
5 Caravan
6 Rival
7 Corsair
8 Loosest
15 Canvasser
16 Ramadan
17 Athwart
18 Pyjamas
19 Spheric
20 Outflow
21 Faraday
23 Rural

76

ACROSS

1 Anthropoid
6 Scow
9 Theodolite
10 Elul
12 Lahore
13 Proximal
15 Handkerchief
18 Lounge-lizard
21 Rock-rose
22 Larynx
24 Nome
25 Delphinium
26 Tarn
27 Attainment

DOWN

1 Attila
2 Teethe
3 Rider Haggard
4 Pelf
5 Intermezzo
7 Colombia
8 Wildlife
11 Exacerbation
14 Adolescent
16 Clarinet
17 Dulcimer
19 Byline
20 Exempt
23 Epha

77

ACROSS

1 Vaughan Williams
9 Regarding
10 Mcgee
11 Indulge
12 Scallop
13 Tit
14 Immerse
17 Arabian
19 Canopus
22 Bellhop
24 Hur
25 Embrace
26 Arbiter
28 Plate
29 Afternoon
30 Rock of Gibraltar

DOWN

1 Virginia creeper
2 Urged
3 Hurdler
4 Naivete
5 Ingesta
6 Lemmata
7 Angel-fish
8 Sleeping partner
15 Mont Blanc
16 Sou
18 Ree
20 Placebo
21 Shebang
22 Bran-tub
23 Liberia
27 Trout

78

ACROSS

1 Follow up
6 Godown
9 Adagio
10 & 11 Battle of Waterloo
11 *See 10*
12 Argyle
13 South-eastern
16 Rallied round
19 Malaga
21 & 23 Dame Kiri Te Kanawa
23 *See 21*
24 Norway
25 Papaya
26 Tasmania

DOWN

2 Oldham
3 Logie
4 Woodlouse
5 Pibroch
6 Gutta
7 Delighted
8 Woodlark
13 Solfatara
14 Abutments
15 Habanera
17 Radiant
18 Argali
20 Adana
22 Karma

79

ACROSS

 1 Talcum
 4 Burgundy
 8 Tarpon
 9 Kilowatt
10 Stickjaw
11 Impair
12 Protocol
13 Hawaii
15 Icarus
18 Pugilism
20 Cognac
21 Doorpost
23 Daiquiri
24 Gawain
25 Mah-Jongg
26 Africa

DOWN

 1 Titus
 2 Capacitor
 3 Muntjac
 4 Bakewell
   pudding
 5 Raleigh
 6 Niagara
 7 Ytterbium
12 Princedom
14 Willpower
16 Anguish
17 Section
19 Georgia
22 Tonga

80

ACROSS

 1 Holst
 4 Howitzer
 8 Corporal
 9 Shanghai
11 Shotton
13 Algeciras
15 Cedars of
   Lebanon
18 Sisyphean
21 Drachma
22 Covenant
24 Artefact
25 Kinkajou
26 Token

DOWN

 1 Hocus-pocus
 2 Larboard
 3 Trottoir
 4 Hals
 5 Irenic
 6 Zither
 7 Raki
10 Highland
12 Napoleon
14 Sand-martin
16 Budapest
17 Noah's ark
19 Severn
20 Panama
22 Cask
23 Tabu

81

ACROSS

 1 Woodchuck
 6 Woden
 9 Tijuana
10 Bagatelle
11 Detente
12 Relaxed
13 Garden of
   England
18 Fuchsia
20 Bermuda
22 Zebra-wood
23 Atavism
24 Gaged
25 Ombudsman

DOWN

 1 Watchdog
 2 Objector
 3 Crayon
 4 Unable
 5 Kedgeree
 6 White-leg
 7 Duplex
 8 Nereid
14 Enslaved
15 Oratorio
16 Aquarium
17 Dragoman
18 Fizgig
19 Coburg
20 Bedaub
21 Roland

88

ACROSS
1 Comanchero
6 MAFF
10 Vinyl
11 Tripitaka
12 Pfennigs
13 Ionic
15 Arshine
17 Earache
19 Protein
21 Pierrot
22 Chang
24 Barbados
27 Inshallah
28 Crane
29 Oyez
30 Prosciutto

DOWN
1 Cova
2 Manifesto
3 Nylon
4 Hittite
5 Reissue
7 Alain
8 Fianchetto
9 Filigree
14 Cappuccino
16 Ideogram
18 Cormorant
20 Nebular
21 Porthos
23 Aisle
25 ASCII
26 Peso

89

ACROSS
1 Grandee
5 Classic
9 Ophthalmologist
10 Corm
11 Agist
12 Akko
15 Insecta
16 Shawnee
17 Malaria
19 Snapper
21 Nero
22 Scrip
23 Warp
26 Gastroenteritis
27 Abscess
28 Cabaret

DOWN
1 Gnocchi
2 Atherosclerosis
3 Dahl
4 Eulogia
5 Croesus
6 Aloe
7 Sticking-plaster
8 Cathode
13 Acorn
14 Japan
17 Managua
18 Archers
19 Sciatic
20 Reposit
24 Cree
25 Crab

90

ACROSS
1 Proverbs
5 Sappho
9 Negatory
10 Bolero
12 Manhattan
13 Imago
14 Saul
16 Primero
19 Strudel
21 Cane
24 Rondo
25 Carbonari
27 Spores
28 Lovelace
29 [one-man
30 Infantas

DOWN
1 Panama
2 Organs
3 Extra
4 Borstal
6 Abolition
7 Pleiades
8 Olorosos
11 Snap
15 Andromeda
17 Espresso
18 Francome
20 Lice
21 Cartoon
22 Basalt
23 Eiders
26 Omega

91

ACROSS

1 Mumbo-jumbo
6 Beeb
9 Spillikins
10 Opus
13 Veloute
15 Norman
16 Oyster
17 Leading question
18 Vienna
20 Bootle
21 Trinket
22 Node
25 Cylindrite
26 Anne
27 Playwright

DOWN

1 Must
2 Mail
3 Oilmen
4 Unknown quantity
5 Benito
7 Expatriate
8 Bushranger
11 Uncle Vanya
12 Armageddon
13 Valiant
14 Eye-spot
19 Argyll
20 Bender
23 Bing
24 Kent

92

ACROSS

1 Holyhead
5 Handel
9 Rabelais
10 Slalom
11 Courting
12 Opiate
14 Stalactite
18 Travelogue
22 Minuet
23 De La Mare
24 Lutein
25 Stardust
26 Scythe
27 Prospero

DOWN

1 Horace
2 Labour
3 Halite
4 Alienation
6 Allspice
7 Dalmatia
8 Lampeter
13 Gloucester
15 Stimulus
16 Mainstay
17 Jeremiah
19 Taurus
20 Danube
21 Dextro

93

ACROSS

7 Freeway
8 Janacek
10 Gerald Ford
11 Tort
12 Pamphlet
14 Rookie
15 Quare Fellow
19 Aegeus
20 Podiatry
22 Neuf
23 Brian Close
25 Runcorn
26 Pelotan

DOWN

1 Freeman
2 Hera
3 Vandal
4 Fal de rol
5 Gastropoda
6 Georgia
9 Port of Spain
13 Pluperfect
16 Rosebery
17 Renegue
18 Preston
21 Daniel
24 Laos

94

ACROSS

7 Ulan Bator
8 Oriel
10 Township
11 Russia
12 Osso
13 Spumante
15 Measles
17 Spiders
20 Amundsen
22 Taps
25 Ankara
26 European
27 Sepal
28 Nicaragua

DOWN

1 Alloa
2 Ananas
3 Rathbone
4 Compass
5 Brassard
6 Hemiptera
9 Urdu
14 Germander
16 Sandarac
18 Peter May
19 Anaemia
21 Shag
23 Poplar
24 Hague

95

ACROSS

1 Armadillo
8 Liechtenstein
11 Iota
12 Ammon
13 Egan
16 Thermos
17 Strange
18 Scallop
20 Poussin
21 Hope
22 Flout
23 Tass
26 Ionian Islands
27 Scarlatti

DOWN

2 Rice
3 Artemis
4 Igneous
5 Lute
6 Littlehampton
7 Virgin Islands
9 Nietzsche
10 Inverness
14 Small
15 Braun
19 Pilsner
20 Prussia
24 Zinc
25 Kant

96

ACROSS

7 Volcano
8 Surtees
10 Stereotype
11 Yoga
12 Bouffant
14 Athena
15 Pharyngitis
19 Biceps
20 Espresso
22 Seth
23 & 26 Montserrat Caballe
25 Riviera
26 See 23

DOWN

1 Pontoon
2 Acer
3 Angola
4 Gujerati
5 Strychnine
6 Yevgeny
9 Ayrton Senna
13 Fahrenheit
16 Rosemary
17 Liberia
18 Assault
21 Pascal
24 Rial

97

ACROSS

7 Fabianism
8 Whelk
10 23 12 & 25 The Prime Of Miss Jean Brodie
11 Thrace
12 *See 10*
13 Indy cars
15 Patrese
17 Avocado
20 Glaucoma
22 Loot
25 *See 10*
26 Chalmers
27 Snell
28 Beardsley

DOWN

1 Dacha
2 Wimple
3 Ancients
4 Asterix
5 Thoracic
6 Electrode
9 Stud
14 Ballerina
16 Roundels
18 Voltaire
19 Catcher
21 Owen
23 *See 10*
24 Greer

98

ACROSS

7 Nick Faldo
8 & 18 Edgar Allan Poe
10 Nebraska
11 Arnica
12 & 19 Myra Hindley
13 Daedalus
15 *See 1*
17 Rameses
20 Paganini
22 Loss
25 Curfew
26 Donleavy
27 & 9 Drury Lane
28 Devonport

DOWN

1 & 15 Nigel Mansell
2 Skerry
3 Marshall
4 Edwards
5 Eden Kane
6 Vancouver
9 *See 27*
14 Kama Sutra
16 Stanford
18 *See 8*
19 See 12
21 Iowa
23 Steppe
24 Ovary

99

ACROSS

1 The Moguls
8 Heath Robinson
11 Dail
12 Athos
13 Avon
16 Madison
17 Samurai
18 Mayfair
20 Corsair
21 Tees
22 Uvula
23 Opus
26 Hilaire Belloc
27 Ascension

DOWN

2 Hite
3 Marston
4 Gibbons
5 Lynx
6 Cecil Day-lewis
7 Wolverhampton
9 Adam Smith
10 & 24 Anti-trust laws
14 Aswan
15 Emery
19 Reverie
20 Celebus
24 *See 10*
25 Alto

100

ACROSS

7 Connery
8 Theorem
10 Noel Coward
11 Cyst
12 Mitchell
14 Sweden
15 Hippocratic
19 France
20 Sillitoe
22 Miro
23 Milan Panic
24 Fleming
25 Conakry

DOWN

1 Borodin
2 Anil
3 Brooke
4 Rhodesia
5 Boccherini
6 Webster
9 Ballycastle
13 Cairngorms
16 Piedmont
17 Braille
18 Moliere
21 London
24 Aral

101

ACROSS

8 Zola
9 Ira
10 Exocet
11 Carpel
12 Ornstein
13 General Pershing
15 Airlift
17 Compost
20 Toulouse Lautrec
23 Turnskin
25 Ibanez
26 19 & 28 George Bernard Shaw
27 Roc
28 *See 26*

DOWN

1 Horace
2 Campbell
3 William Faulkner
4 Jaloppy
5 Leonardo da Vinci
6 Hootch
7 Yeti
14 Nis
16 Ibo
18 Petrassi
19 *See 26 across*
21 Lanark
22 Evejar
24 Ulex

102

ACROSS

7 Analgesic
8 Blunt
10 Pancreas
11 Luther
12 Otto
13 Navarino
15 Anarchy
17 Sophist
20 Koestler
22 Iowa
25 Gemini
26 Domenico
27 Vichy
28 Canaletto

DOWN

1 Snead
2 Placet
3 Behemoth
4 Ginseng
5 Plutarch
6 Inverness
9 Slav
14 Indonesia
16 Respighi
18 Opium war
19 Trudeau
21 Lair
23 Wankel
24 Scott

103

ACROSS

1 Alpenstock
6 Clef
9 Dick Turpin
10 Impi
13 Rake-off
15 Indian
16 Safari
17 Hansel and Gretel
18 Thalia
20 Gander
21 Timothy
22 Eros
25 Objections
26 Toys
27 Escapology

DOWN

1 Aida
2 Pick
3 Nathan
4 Threepenny Opera
5 Cliffs
7 Lammastide
8 Fritillary
11 High Street
12 Odontalogy
13 Rarebit
14 Fairway
19 Airbus
20 Ghetto
23 Polo
24 Espy

104

ACROSS

1 Caravanserai
8 Dim
9 Liassic
11 Look you
12 Nylghau
13 Fytte
14 Elm Street
16 Yokemates
18 Khmer
20 Indians
22 Classic
23 Erewhon
25 Ell
26 As true a lover

DOWN

1 Comfort
2 Restyle
3 Vol-au-vent
4 Nylon
5 Epaulet
6 Ass
7 Idol of my life
10 Count Dracula
15 Music hall
17 Meacher
18 Kharkov
19 Masseur
21 Singe
24 Ess

105

ACROSS

1 Once upon a time
10 Almanac
11 Optical
12 Ra-ra
13 Milly
14 Adze
17 Pahlavi
18 Seismal
19 Impasto
22 Buttons
24 Tilt
25 Scrip
26 Tarn
29 Narwhal
30 Dahlias
31 Typographical

DOWN

2 Nomarch
3 Eons
4 Puccini
5 Noodles
6 Tati
7 Macadam
8 Hairsplitting
9 Sleeplessness
15 Balsa
16 Pinto
20 Palfrey
21 Oscular
22 Build up
23 Ocarina
27 Shoo
28 Thai

106

ACROSS

1 Chainsaws
9 Thuggee
10 Ribston
11 Ass
12 & 4 Tom
   Stoppard
13 Chiropody
15 Isolates
16 Condor
18 Edition
21 Pinkie
24 Tipstaff
26 Afrikaner
27 Ill
28 Out
29 Minaret
30 Genoese
31 Rain-gauge

DOWN

2 Heigh-ho
3 Insured
4 *See 12 across*
5 Strays
6 Mussolini
7 Agitato
8 Seamy side
14 Distaff
16 Cartridge
17 Oestrogen
19 Ophidian
20 Opaline
22 Niagara
23 Iceberg
25 Father

107

ACROSS

1 Maastricht
6 Okra
9 Olive
10 Ectoplasm
12 Timpani
13 Bring
15 Hatband
17 Ellwand
19 Premium
21 Gestapo
22 Tessa
24 Chapati
27 Colosseum
28 Hotel
29 Soya
30 Reproduced

DOWN

1 Moor
2 Aristotle
3 Therm
4 Ireland
5 Hittite
7 Khaki
8 Armageddon
11 Pobbles
14 Chopsticks
16 Animals
18 Atavistic
20 Machete
21 Grammar
23 Sally
25 Aphid
26 Plod

108

ACROSS

1 Mumbles
5 Tap-room
9 Llanero
10 Curator
11 Ellesmere
12 Igloo
13 Nasal
15 Anno mundi
17 Cabriolet
19 Natal
22 Nahum
23 Staying on
25 Pomatum
26 Implant
27 Snaffle
28 Litotes

DOWN

1 Malvern
2 Measles
3 Leeds
4 Stonewall
5 Tache
6 Persimmon
7 Ortolan
8 Marconi
14 Leitmotif
16 Nathaniel
17 Canopus
18 Bohemia
20 Taggart
21 Lengths
23 Somme
24 Input

109

ACROSS

1 & 9 Christopher Wren
9 *See 1*
10 Cote d'argent
11 Thor
14 Kingdom
16 Albumen
17 Meuse
18 Loin
19 Pooh
20 Obeah
22 Toccata
23 Maracas
24 Neon
28 Empirically
29 Etui
30 Ann Veronica

DOWN

2 Hook
3 Idem
4 Transom
5 Page
6 Ennoble
7 Graham Gooch
8 Enfranchise
12 Skeleton key
13 Anvil Chorus
15 Melba
16 Assam
20 Ottoman
21 Harrier
25 Kiev
26 Pawn
27 Flic

110

ACROSS

1 Tulliver
5 Smee
9 Larboard
10 Anodes
11 To A Mouse
12 Floral
14 Possession
18 Jack Horner
22 Louvre
23 Off-drive
24 Artist
25 Skittles
26 Reel
27 Pear-drop

DOWN

2 Lariat
3 Isopod
4 Earls Court
6 Mona Lisa
7 Endermic
8 Rosalind
9 Lute
13 Isle of Skye
15 Djellaba
16 Accustom
17 Pharisee
19 Editor
20 Miller
21 Lees

111

ACROSS

5 Relish
8 Imperial
9 Ascetic
10 Dante
11 Repechage
13 Rhetoric
14 Tandem
17 Eta
19 Tin
20 Liaise
23 Ornament
26 & 5 Christina Rossetti
28 Uncle
29 Gabriel
30 Cubiform
31 Glamis

DOWN

1 Pindar
2 Spinnet
3 Free votes
4 Safari
5 *See 26*
6 Leech
7 Shingles
12 Ecu
15 Andalusia
16 Highball
18 Tent-pegs
21 Don
22 Reactor
24 Radius
25 Therms
27 Ihram

112

ACROSS

1 Embroidery
9 Coda
10 Isle of Dogs
11 Hacker
12 Box kite
15 Sampler
16 Aback
17 Erne
18 Cran
19 Antra
21 Euphony
22 Erasmus
24 Proust
27 Oligarchic
28 Naif
29 Yarborough

DOWN

2 Musk
3 Reebok
4 Infanta
5 Ebor
6 Yashmak
7 Cockalorum
8 Fairy-rings
12 Bee-keeping
13 Xenophobia
14 Ebony
15 Score
19 Anatomy
20 Arapaho
23 Sancho
25 Pier
26 Ming

113

ACROSS

1 Henry Purcell
9 Holster
10 Ukulele
11 Ghee
12 Lemur
13 Dill
16 Eunuchs
17 Younger
18 Tartare
21 Regents
23 Aids
24 Percy
25 Emir
28 Eclipse
29 Treason
30 Robert Graves

DOWN

1 Holbein
2 Nits
3 Yorkers
4 Uruguay
5 Coup
6 Leeming
7 The Great Lakes
8 Neil Armstrong
14 Eclat
15 Fungi
19 Rodolfo
20 Element
21 Richter
22 Nemesis
26 Epee
27 Derv

114

ACROSS

1 Clapboard
9 Brunel
10 Ogden Nash
11 Peewit
12 Ligaments
13 Moloch
17 Goa
19 Hillary
20 Cashier
21 Pie
23 Really
27 Leicester
28 Harris
29 Saltpetre
30 Lister
31 Edelweiss

DOWN

2 Loggia
3 Pre-fab
4 Ounces
5 Risotto
6 Freehouse
7 Snowdonia
8 Fletchers
14 Churchill
15 Albatross
16 Gauleiter
17 Gyp
18 Ace
22 Ireland
24 Acetal
25 Essene
26 Hearts

115

ACROSS
1 Cybernetics
8 Brandenburg
11 Lark
12 Plum
13 Cabrera
15 Madison
16 Ninon
17 Vein
18 Yogi
19 Caleb
21 Leghorn
22 Decibel
23 Esau
26 Arid
27 Granite city
28 Plagiostome

DOWN
2 York
3 Einkorn
4 Noel
5 Tibetan
6 Carp
7 Black Velvet
8 Brobdingnag
9 Glastonbury
10 Amontillado
14 Aidan
15 Moped
19 Crannog
20 Bear-cat
24 Ural
25 Otto
26 Atom

116

ACROSS
1 Hudson
4 Bessemer
8 Gothic
9 Laburnum
10 Eclipsed
11 Repton
12 Zugzwang
13 Ararat
15 Callas
18 Ramequin
20 Evvoia
21 Mackinaw
23 Martello
24 Dotard
25 Nattered
26 Milton

DOWN
1 Hague
2 Schnitzel
3 Nicosia
4 Bull-dog
  Drummond
5 Siberia
6 Monster
7 Remington
12 Zuckerman
14 Acquittal
16 Leveret
17 Stapler
19 Macadam
22 Woden

117

ACROSS
1 Cowes
4 Mortimer
8 Raillery
9 Abrasion
11 October
13 Hollywood
15 Northanger
  Abbey
18 Saltpetre
21 Racemic
22 Pacifist
24 Ensnarer
25 Handrail
26 Delve

DOWN
1 Coriolanus
2 Whistler
3 Saltbush
4 Maya
5 Treaty
6 Merino
7 Roan
10 Believer
12 Rhinitis
14 D'Oyly Carte
16 Arachnid
17 Balmoral
19 Lichen
20 Puffer
22 Posh
23 Tell

118

ACROSS
 1 Eggplant
 9 Rossetti
10 Ares
11 Quarterstaff
13 Typecast
15 Stigma
16 Peel
17 Canto
18 Orff
20 Darwin
21 Trifocal
23 Charterhouse
26 Tees
27 Radiator
28 Platypus

DOWN
 2 Gargoyle
 3 Pasque-flower
 4 Ankara
 5 Trot
 6 Espresso
 7 Etna
 8 Riff-raff
12 Trigonometry
14 Tenet
16 Pedicure
17 Concerto
19 Flambeau
22 Iguana
24 Aida
25 Harp

119

ACROSS
 1 Cherubic
 6 Bodice
 9 Tarmac
10 & 11 David and
    Jonathan
11 See 10
12 Lucian
13 Cantabrigian
16 Footplateman
19 Pharos
21 Jeroboam
23 Hula-Hula
24 Nestor
25 Isolde
26 Antilles

DOWN
 2 Head-on
 3 Rumba
 4 Bacchanal
 5 Cadenza
 6 Bevel
 7 Dodecagon
 8 Cinnabar
13 Caterwaul
14 Rembrandt
15 Jodhpurs
17 Tijuana
18 Parole
20 Saute
22 Basil

120

ACROSS
 1 Zebedee
 5 Cambric
 9 Nomad
10 Thornbill
11 The Tempest
12 Wren
14 Disadvantage
18 Saul of Tarsus
21 Toby
22 Folkestone
25 Ellipsoid
26 Total
27 Margery
28 Surinam

DOWN
 1 Zenith
 2 Bumper
 3 Didgeridoo
 4 Estop
 5 Crossover
 6 Manx
 7 Railroad
 8 Colander
13 Inquisitor
15 Anthology
16 Isotherm
17 Quibbler
19 Boston
20 Vellum
23 Kudos
24 Opie